THE
AMERICAN
POLITICAL
SYSTEM
A RADICAL APPROACH

Edward S. Greenberg

★ **Custom Edition for Foothill College** ★

Taken from:

The American Political System: A Radical Approach, Fifth Edition
by Edward S. Greenberg

PEARSON
Custom
Publishing

PEARSON
Longman

Taken from:

The American Political System: A Radical Approach, Fifth Edition
by Edward S. Greenberg
Copyright © 1989 by Edward S. Greenberg
Published by Longman
A Pearson Education Company
New York, New York 10010

Printed in the United States of America

10 9 8 7 6 5 4 3 2 1

ISBN 0-536-56109-5

2007480105

JK

Please visit our web site at *www.pearsoncustom.com*

PEARSON CUSTOM PUBLISHING
501 Boylston Street, Suite 900, Boston, MA 02116
A Pearson Education Company

For Martha, Josh, and Nathaniel,
with affection.

Preface

This edition has been revised to lend greater coherence to its main line of argument and to incorporate the most lasting legacies of what some have called the Reagan Revolution. I have cut material from previous editions that is tangential to my main point of view, and I have woven the thread of the argument throughout each of the chapters. I have done this by continuously addressing the interrelationships of American politics, American capitalism, social justice, and democracy. I have also attempted to assess the implications for American life and politics of America's relative decline in the world economy.

Taken from *The American Political System: A Radical Approach,* Fifth Edition
by Edward S. Greenberg

Table

of Contents

Letter written by Jacob L. Vowel shortly before he died of suffocation in the 1902 Fraterville, Tennessee, mine disaster

Part

I

Overview and

Analytic Approach

In this section, the reader is introduced to the principal themes of the text and to the theoretical materials that will serve as guideposts in our trek through the sometimes confusing landscape of American political, economic, and social life.

1

Capitalism

and American Politics:

An Introduction to

Central Themes

AN INTRODUCTION:
DEATH, MAYHEM, AND PUBLIC POLICY

☐ Of the butchers and floorsmen, the beef boners and trimmers, and all those who
used knives, you could scarcely find a person who had the use of his thumb; time
and time again the base of it had been slashed, 'til it was a mere lump of flesh
against which the man pressed the knife to hold it. The hands of these men
would be criss-crossed with cuts, until you could no longer pretend to count
them or to trace them. They would have no nails—they had worn them off
pulling hides; their knuckles were swollen so that their fingers spread out like a
fan. There were men who worked in the cooking rooms, in the midst of steam
and sickening odors, by artificial light; in these rooms the germs of tuberculosis
might live for two years, but the supply was renewed every hour. There were the
beef-luggers, who carried two-hundred-pound quarters into the refrigerator-
cars; a fearful kind of work, that began at four o'clock in the morning, and that
wore out the most powerful men in a few years. There were those who worked in
the chilling rooms, and whose special disease was rheumatism; the time limit
that a man could work in the chilling rooms was said to be five years. There were
the wool-pluckers, whose hands went to pieces even sooner than the hands of the
pickle men; for the pelts of the sheep had to be painted with acid to loosen the
wool, and then the pluckers had to pull out this wool with their bare hands, 'til
the acid had eaten their fingers off. There were those who made the tins for the
canned meat; and their hands, too, were a maze of cuts, and each cut represented
a chance for blood poisoning. Some worked at the stamping machines, and it
was very seldom that one could work long there at the pace that was set, and not
give out and forget himself, and have a part of his hand chopped off. There were
the "hoisters," as they were called, whose task it was to press the lever which
lifted the dead cattle off the floor. They ran along upon a rafter, peering down

through the damp and the steam; and as old Durham's architects had not built the killing room for the convenience of the hoisters, at every few feet they would have to stoop under a beam, say four feet above the one they ran on; which got them into the habit of stooping, so that in a few years they would be walking like chimpanzees. Worst of any, however, were the fertilizer men, and those who served in the cooking rooms. These people could not be shown to the visitor—for the odor of a fertilizer man would scare any ordinary visitor at a hundred yards, and as for the other men, who worked in tank rooms full of steam, and in some of which there were open vats near the level of the floor, their peculiar trouble was that they fell into the vats; and when they were fished out, there was never enough of them left to be worth exhibiting—sometimes they would be overlooked for days, 'til all but the bones of them had gone out to the world as Durham's Pure Leaf Lard! [1]

☐ You may wonder why asbestos workers walk backwards. They don't always walk backwards. It is only going upstairs. They are so short of breath that after two steps they have to sit down. It is easier to go up a flight of stairs backwards than walking up. It is a terrible way to die. [2]

☐ REPRESENTATIVE DANIELS: Why did these people who work on the farm become sick?

MRS. OLIVERAS: Because the day before, they spray the field. The next morning they put the people in the field and they took about six of these workers to the doctor and the doctor talked to the people. He said they get sunstroke. The people are going to get sunstroke by seven o'clock in the morning? [3]

☐ A young sprayer was found dead in the field in the tractor which had been pulling his spray-rig. He had been pouring and mixing parathion concentrate into the spray-rig tank. Parathion has an estimated fatal dose of about nine drops orally and thirty-two drops dermally. In the process of mixing the concentrate, the worker contaminated his gloves inside and out. He rested his gloved hands on his trousers as he pulled the rig to apply the spray. Parathion was absorbed through the skin of his hand and thighs. He began to vomit, an early symptom of parathion poisoning. He could not remove his respirator and he aspirated the vomitus. The diagnosis of poisoning was confirmed by postmortem cholinesterase tests. [4]

☐ When I went to work, I was in good health, I thought, as a boy of that age. I could get out and run and play and wasn't bothered any. So I went to work in the carding department. . . .

The mill then was much more open than today. But I began to notice when I would play I couldn't breathe as good as I could before I went to work. Being young and not thinking much about it, I kept on going at it, and finally I married and then I was hooked to keep on working.

So I kept on working and my breathing kept on getting worse. I went along, and I got to the point where I would just cough and sometimes hang over a can and cough and become nauseated in my stomach, and I began to be bothered about my condition.

I decided that maybe this dust was doing that. I started taking a little bit closer watch on that and taking a little closer check on it. I have seen three-hundred-watt electric bulbs in the plant that I worked in where the ceiling was high, and they looked like they were red and not much more than a twenty-five watt bulb. When the mill would run two or three days, you could look up and see the light bulbs and they looked like they were red. You could get over by the window where the sun was shining through, and the dust particles were so thick when you looked into that sunshine that it looked like you could just reach out and grab a handful of it. . . .

Apparently, people would look at me and say that I am in very good physical shape. All of my life I have been very active, but now I am short of breath, and I can't do anything. I get so short of breath and so weak, I can hardly go.

As far as I see things, and as far as the doctor says, I will be like this as long as I live.[5]

☐ He often had to clean out large tanks that had been used to store toxic chemicals. He sometimes got dizzy and groggy at work. Like a good soldier, he would continue to work and not complain. Then one day he blacked out at home. He began to spit blood. . . . Jim began to develop skin lesions all over his body.

Jim took off time from work during the worst onslaughts of dizziness, but he went back as soon as he possibly could. He had a family to support. At work one day, the foreman told him to climb inside a particularly noxious chemical tank and clean it out. Jim refused, saying that there wasn't enough breathable air in it. The foreman told Jim that if he didn't do what he was told he'd be laid off for ten days. This was not a union shop and Jim had absolutely no recourse. "I got a family and the rent to pay and my phone and light and my transportation to and from work. So I went ahead and cleaned the tank because I couldn't afford to be off. I had four kids at home then." His only protection was a mask that didn't really stop any of the toxic fumes.

By late 1979 Jim was unable to work any longer. He just couldn't breathe if he was on his feet for any length of time. Schwinn fired him since he wouldn't work. Jim's medical insurance was dependent on his working at Schwinn. He lost the insurance when he lost the job.[6]

☐ "Stepan Golab, a 59-year-old illegal immigrant from Poland, worked for a year stirring tanks of sodium cyanide at the Film Recovery Services plant in Elk Grove, Illinois. On February 10, 1983, Golab became dizzy from the cyanide fumes, went into convulsions, and died."[7] After his death, the Occupational Safety and Health Administration inspected the plant and levied fines of $4,855 for twenty safety violations. OSHA later reduced the fine by 50 percent. Later court testimony revealed that plant officials had known of the extreme dangers involved in the film recovery operations and had failed to take even minimal precautions to protect the health and safety of their workers.

☐ "Nothing's more dangerous in all the world than logging," said . . . Bill Holloway, a one-time timber cutter who remembers seeing a worker drop a chain saw on his thigh. "Cut right through the leg and left him sputtering there in shock. I gave him a cussing, saying he wasn't man enough to walk out of these woods, but that was just to divert his attention until we could get help."[8]

☐ On November 20, 1968, at 5:25 A.M., a massive explosion at Consolidation Coal Company's No. 9 mine at Farmington, West Virginia, snuffed out the lives of seventy-eight miners. According to the experts, the explosion was detonated by a lethal combination of methane gas (the mine, strangely enough, was situated above a massive natural gas field) and high concentrations of coal dust caused by inadequate safety procedures on the part of Consolidation Coal. The No. 9 mine had been found in violation of government rock dusting requirements in every inspection made in the five years previous to the disaster at Farmington.[9] One federal mine inspector reported that during his inspection of the mine the previous August, he had reported four serious violations of federal safety laws.[10] Yet, in the immediate aftermath of the disaster, public and private officials rushed to Farmington to absolve Consolidation Coal and its parent company, Continental Oil, from any moral responsibility or legal culpability.

"We must remember that this is a hazardous business and that what has occurred here is one of the hazards of being a miner."

—Gov. Hulett C. Smith of West Virginia

"Unfortunately—we don't understand why these things happen—but they do happen. . . . The company here has done all in its power to make this a safe mine."

—J. Cordell Moore, Assistant Secretary of the Interior

"If the mine was unsafe, we would have stopped operations and that's all there is to it."

—William Parks, Bureau of Mines, Department of the Interior

"I share the grief. I've lost relatives in a mine explosion. . . . This happens to be one of the better companies, as far as cooperation with our union and safety is concerned."

—Tony Boyle, President, United Mine Workers

"Whatever is our fate, may we accept it."

—The Rev. John Barnes, Farmington, West Virginia

Working miners, on the other hand, were under no illusions about the cause of the disaster:

"It's been filled with gas . . . something was bound to happen." [11]

—Ora Haught, miner for twenty-seven years

BUSINESS, GOVERNMENT, WORKERS, AND THE WORKPLACE

Work, it seems, is hazardous to one's health. The overall figures on the scope of the hazard in the United States are staggering. It is estimated [12] that on average, over 5 million Americans are injured on the job annually, nearly 400,000 contract *new* cases of disabling occupational disease, more than 100,000 die from such diseases, and 15,000 die in accidents. Ninety thousand die annually from cancers contracted at work. [13] This level of carnage must strike even the most casual observer as the equivalent of full-scale warfare in its effects. More Americans died from job accidents or from work-related diseases annually, in fact, than were killed in combat action during the same years in Korea or Vietnam. [14]

If the levels of work-related death, injury, and disease in the United States are distressing when seen in isolation, they are even more distressing when compared to those of other industrialized nations. That is, while the job-safety record of the United States has improved over the years, it still seriously lags behind that of other nations. Official statistics reported by the International Labor Organization in 1986 show the United States to have suffered twice the rate (per one million

TABLE 1.1   The Most Dangerous Industries in the United States

ANNUAL FATALITIES PER 100,000 WORKERS, 1980–1984	
Mining	30.1
Construction	23.1
Agriculture, forestry, and fishing	20.3
Transportation, communication, and public utilities	19.5

SOURCE: *The New York Times*, January 10, 1988, p. E5. Based on data from the National Institute for Occupational Safety and Health. Copyright © 1988 by The New York Times Company. Reprinted by permission.

man-hours) of job-related fatalities as the Netherlands, 50 percent more than Great Britain, and 40 percent more than Sweden.[15] Comparative rates of work-related death (which include death caused by diseases and debilitating injuries) show an even gloomier picture: One scholar estimates that United States rates are fourteen times greater than Sweden's and twenty times greater than Great Britain's.[16]

Mining is particularly dangerous, especially in the United States, where death and injury rates are among the highest in the western world. The United States' violent death rate in mining, for instance, is almost four times greater than that of Great Britain and six times that of the Netherlands, despite the fact that American mines enjoy uniquely favorable conditions—"seams which are thicker, more horizontal, closer to the surface, and less gaseous"[17] than those found in most other parts of the world. Farmington was but a dramatic instance of the generally bloody history of the mining industry. Though records are not entirely accurate, one student of mining history estimates that "in the 100 years that partial records of fatal mine accidents have been kept . . . more than 120,000 men have died violently in coal mines, an average of 100 every month for a century."[18] By all estimates, mining is the most dangerous occupation in the United States (see Table 1.1), with annual fatalities far ahead of the competition's. Even more coal miners die annually from "black-lung" disease contracted during their work years. Among miners over sixty years of age, the natural death rate is eight times that of any other industrial occupation; almost all such deaths are traceable to "black lung." Well over 100,000 today suffer its effects. It is not a pretty way to live or die:

> I was a coal miner for thirty-nine years. I went to work in the coal mine when I was thirteen years old. Out of the thirty-nine years, I served five years in the armed forces in World War II. I had to quit work on account of pneumoconiosis, or black lung, whichever you want to call it, and I was advised by ten different doctors to quit work, that I am not supposed even to drive my car. I am not supposed to go fishing. I am not supposed to do anything according to the depositions from the doctors. I have, and I am supposed to fall dead any time. I never sleep at night. I stay awake and sleep on the average about two and one-half hours a day, and most of that is sitting in a chair. I never had any pleasure out of life at all since I had to quit the mine. On eight different occasions I was hauled out of the mine because I was passing out because I could not get enough air to breathe.[19]

Despite the hue and cry raised against government regulation in recent years by business, the history of government involvement in questions of job safety has been one of general neglect until forced by workers, unions, and public opinion to take remedial action, followed by indifferent enforcement of the law as public awareness recedes. Concerned about the prerogatives of business and sensitive to the need for corporate profitability, political leaders have turned their attention to the hazards of the workplace with the greatest reluctance and only after years of pressure from workers, unions, and reformers.

Take mine safety as an example. Government has done less than would be expected, given the scale of the safety problem, because mining industry/government relations have generally been collusive and cooperative rather than antagonistic. In West Virginia, in eastern Kentucky, and in eastern Tennessee, where most deep mining is done, the coal companies literally *were* the government for at least three generations. In the early days of the industry, most miners lived in company towns owned, organized, and closely managed by the coal companies. In more modern times, coal company power and money—particularly with local populations largely immobilized by exhaustion, poverty, and fear—have been the guiding forces in selecting both elected and appointed officials, particularly county judges, sheriffs, and tax commissioners (to say nothing of senators, representatives, and governors).[20] Selection of sheriffs and tax commissioners is particularly important to mine corporations: sheriffs police the often unruly miners,

Slow death: a black-lung victim

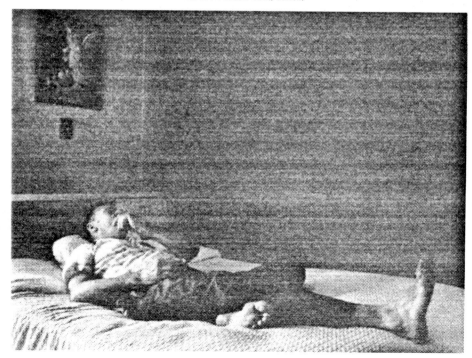

and tax commissioners keep coal company taxes at a minimum. Needless to say, such officials have not been overeager to either propose or execute safety legislation.

The record of the federal government is considerably better, yet the pattern of cooperation with business is again apparent. Thus, a number of mine safety laws dot the statute books, but these laws have not brought the level of safety in American mines up to international standards. Federal mine safety legislation usually follows a predictable sequence of events: A major mining tragedy rouses mine workers and the general public; mine safety legislation is pushed through Congress. Characteristically, this legislation is rife with loopholes and industry-favoring compromises, or it is unenforceable or simply unenforced. For instance, one act passed in 1941 gave the Bureau of Mines power to designate equipment as "permissible" or "nonpermissible" but no power to control the use of such equipment. Between 1941 and 1952, when the legislation was amended, at least half of all mine explosions, resulting in 835 deaths, were caused by the electric arcs of "nonpermissible" equipment.[21] The amended mine safety legislation of 1952 included a "grandfather" clause by which companies could continue to use nonpermissible equipment already in place or on order. Much of this equipment, now rebuilt two or three times, is still in use. The 1952 act also exempted from federal jurisdiction any deaths and injury not related to major disasters. Most accidents and deaths result from roof collapses at the working face of the mine and involve but a handful of miners at any one time.

The public outcry over the Farmington disaster caused mine safety legislation to be strengthened considerably. Yet, though the safety performance of the industry greatly improved during the 1970s and 1980s, American deep-pit coal mining remained among the most dangerous in the industrialized western world.[22] This was not so much because of formal deficiencies in the language of the Mine Safety Act of 1969 but because of deficiencies in enforcement:

1. Not enough federal mine inspectors were employed by the Mine Safety Administration to accomplish the safety goals specified in the law, especially after President Carter froze the budget for hiring inspectors in 1978. The situation became even worse under President Reagan.
2. Inspections of mines were usually announced in advance, giving mine companies time to temporarily fix or to disguise unsafe practices.
3. Inspectors rarely imposed solutions to unsafe conditions, typically negotiating compromise settlements with mining corporations instead.
4. Maximum fines allowable under the law are almost never imposed. Consolidation Coal was assessed $2,872,317 for 14,090 violations of the Mine Safety Act of 1969 between 1969 and 1972 but paid only $896,355.[23]
5. Although they have the legal power to shut down an operation, federal mine inspectors rarely do so, even when faced with flagrant, repeated, and demonstrably dangerous violations.

Given these shortcomings in the 1969 Coal Mine Health and Safety Act and its enforcement, disasters such as the one at Farmington have remained an unwelcome yet persistent factor in the mining industry. On March 9, 1976, twenty-six miners were killed in an explosion at the Scotia Coal Company mine in Oven Fork, Kentucky. The explosion was triggered by the electric arc of an archaic locomotive operating in a shaft in which illegal ventilation practices had caused lethal concentrations of methane gas. Investigators also noted a consistent failure to comply with monitoring and inspection requirements. Between 1970 and the time of the explosion, Scotia had been cited for 855 violations of federal standards. Yet in the face of this history of violations of the law and in the wake of the disaster, the chief of the Division of Safety for the Mine Enforcement and Safety Administration was moved to say that "Scotia stands tall in the industry" in matters of mine safety. Is it any wonder that between the Farmington and Scotia disasters over 1,000 miners lost their lives despite the existence of the Mine Safety Act?[24]

Apparently, even these less-than-perfect efforts by the federal government to ensure the safety of coal miners was too much for the Reagan administration. In an attempt to end what Mine Safety and Health Administration director F. B. Ford had termed the "traditional adversarial relationship" between government and the coal operators, the Reagan administration further decimated the enforcement of the mine safety laws: The enforcement budget was drastically cut, the size of the inspection staff was reduced, fewer inspections were carried out, the number of citations dwindled, and the average amount of fines for safety violations shrank steadily. Director Ford is even reported to have promoted a scheme whereby the coal companies would police themselves and certify on their own that their operations were safe. This war on business regulation had the effect of seriously eroding working conditions for American underground coal miners. By the end of Reagan's first term, deaths in this sector of the mining industry were at their highest level since the early 1970s.[25] At the end of 1984, just before Christmas, twenty-seven miners died in a fire at the Wilberg Mine in Utah caused by a spark igniting accumulated methane gas.

Much the same story can be told of the Occupational Safety and Health Act signed into law by President Nixon on December 29, 1970. Passed amid high hopes and florid rhetoric, the legislation was, in fact, less than it seemed. It represented an important step toward the protection of employees in the workplace to the extent that it mandated "the greatest possible protection of the safety and health of the affected employee," required employers to provide a workplace "free from recognized hazards," gave individual workers and union locals a role in setting and enforcing standards, and granted OSHA the authority to inspect, issue citations for violations, and propose penalties; but business recalcitrance, legislative loopholes, and inconsistent enforcement have served to disappoint expectations in this seemingly revolutionary legislation. While rates of work-related death, injury, and disease have declined since the passage of the Occupational Safety and Health Act, the decline has been less than expected and less than what is possible when compared to rates from other nations.

The inclination of the Nixon administration was to depend on voluntary compliance with the legislation and soft persuasion, and to that end it appointed businesspeople to head OSHA and its major divisions. Furthermore, OSHA based its inspections in its first years on safety standards formulated by the various industry trade associations, organizations that one would expect would be solicitous of employee concerns. Given the paucity of inspectors, only a tiny fraction of workplaces were visited by OSHA every year, and in those cases where violations were noted, fines were generally so small that most companies simply absorbed them as a minor cost of production. Between 1971 and 1975, in fact, the *average* penalty imposed by OSHA came to a mere $25. Business enterprises also became quite adept at contesting and delaying the process of inspection, citation, and penalty, and thus at minimizing the need to rectify hazardous conditions, through an elaborate appeals process. Many companies simply refused to comply and forced OSHA and complaining employees to seek redress in lengthy and costly court procedures. Workers thus found themselves at a great disadvantage, standing virtually alone against a battery of corporate lawyers. Without the desire or the ability to tackle the major violators of health and safety, OSHA was reduced to mainly writing "nit-picking" standards like the infamous ones mandating the design and use of toilet facilities.

During the administration of Jimmy Carter, who, it seems, owed his election to the labor union vote, and under the leadership of Eula Bingham, OSHA entered a brief period in which it enforced more rigorously than before the letter and the spirit of the law by issuing more stringent standards, increasing the rate of inspections, and slightly stiffening penalties. The result was a small yet significant improvement in the wholesomeness of the American work environment. Needless to say, the increased cost and inconvenience encouraged business leaders and their allies to launch a concerted and highly effective campaign to gut OSHA. The attack came from many directions. Corporate spokespersons complained about economic inefficiencies and costs to their enterprises caused by OSHA requirements and bureaucratic bungling,[26] and with their considerable resources were soon able to dominate the debate on the nation's airwaves and in its corridors of government power. To these public relations activities were joined the not-so-subtle threats by some corporations to move their production facilities to Third World nations less concerned about the safety of their workforce. Hand in hand with these attacks came the widespread practice of noncooperation (in terms of reporting data, opening enterprises to inspection, complying with directives), as well as a series of successful court challenges to the right of OSHA safety inspectors to enter the workplace unannounced.

In a very short period of time, the ground under the work safety movement had shifted dramatically. By the end of the Carter administration, OSHA officials had begun to retreat before the counterattack of the business community and to speak in terms of relying more on market forces and less on government coercion as a means to encourage healthy workplaces. By 1980, a series of measures with broad bipartisan support were introduced in the Congress designed to restrict the standard-setting, inspection, and enforcement machinery of the Occupational Safety and Health Administration. Under the openly pro-business regime of Ronald Reagan, the retreat within OSHA was given further impetus by severe cuts in the OSHA budget, by the new requirement that all regulations be subjected to "cost-benefit" analysis (initiated under President Carter), by a slowdown in the process of setting safety standards, and by appointment of agency leadership hostile to the agency's mission. Reagan's OSHA director, Thorne

Auchter, for instance, was a Florida construction company executive whose company had been repeatedly cited for safety violations by OSHA. He gained immediate fame by ordering the destruction of 100,000 copies of an OSHA booklet on "brown lung," which he found to be offensive and biased in favor of labor.

In short order, then, OSHA had been tamed, confined to activities that could, without too much exaggeration, be termed cosmetic. Leon Kruchten, for one, an electrician at the Oscar Mayer plant in Madison, Wisconsin, can attest to the change of OSHA into a "cooperative regulator" (Auchter's apt term). Sustaining major injuries while working at the Oscar Mayer plant because of a surge of 13,000 volts through his body, Kruchten received some satisfaction from an initial OSHA ruling in 1983 that Oscar Mayer's unsafe working conditions warranted a citation for a "serious" violation and a fine of $640. After consulting with company and union representatives, the citation was changed to "nonserious" and the fine was rescinded.[27] The thinking of the new OSHA was captured in a memo written by the chief attorney of the Department of Labor advising Auchter to loosen enforcement of the safety laws: "The relatively low profile of enforcement activities allows greater flexibility and avoids adverse public reaction."[28]

THE ORIENTATION OF THE TEXT

You may be wondering by now what this extended discussion of occupational death, disease, and injury has to do with a textbook on American government and politics. To put it simply, it has *everything* to do with American government and politics; in its many tragic details may be found the essence of our political life, broadly and properly understood. In it we may discern the reality of business control of the workplace and of the conditions of daily existence of most Americans; the treatment of citizens of a democratic country as mere factors of production; the vast extent of the economic, political, and social role of concentrated private economic power; the close collaboration of business and governments at all levels in the United States; the pro-corporate bias in the letter and the administration of the law; the public policy continuities between Democratic and Republican administrations through the years; and the unequal distribution of political power. The various stories of death and injury on the job and the government response to these problems set out at the beginning of this chapter are, then, paradigmatic of the American system and a particularly dramatic way to introduce you to the central concerns and viewpoints of this book. The remainder of the book is, in some respects, merely a generalization from these examples to other aspects of American life. They graphically indicate the themes and concepts that will recur with some frequency in these pages: the nature of business enterprise, the relationship of business to government, the distribution of power and privilege in America, and the living conditions of working Americans. They open the way as well to a consideration of broader questions: What is capitalism and what are its implications for social and political life? How do the major institutions of economic and political life relate to each other? How do economic factors limit possibilities of political choice? How do political decisions affect economic organization and performance? What is the nature of democratic citizenship in a modern society where political, economic, and social power and influence are unevenly distributed?

What is unusual about the analysis in this book is that I consider political and governmental processes not in splendid isolation, but only as they are imbedded in and interact with an identifiable social structure and a particular kind of economic system. In fact, social structure and economy are treated prior to government and politics in this book because of my belief that together they determine the nature of the social problems with which government must deal, the range of permissible options for government policy makers, and the distribution of political power and influence. In other words, I approach the understanding of normal politics (elections, representation, public opinion, and the like) only after I grapple with the problem of understanding the structure, operation, and implications of American capitalism.[29]

At a more concrete level, I am interested in this text in the general patterns of distribution of *social rewards and decision-making power* in American life, and in *the role that government and politics play in determining the shape of these distributions*. The text is organized mainly around the question raised by political scientist Harold Lasswell many years ago: "Who Gets What, When, and How?" In the attempt to answer this general question, the analysis in this text will focus on the following questions:

The distribution of social rewards and burdens:

1. How are wealth, income, shelter, health, security, legal justice, political rights, and the like distributed in American life?
2. What is the role of the capitalist economy in determining these patterns of distribution?
3. What is the role of government and politics in determining these distributions? What are the distributional implications of the vast and varied activities of government in the United States?

The distribution of social decision-making power:

1. Who or what decides the agenda of American politics and government?
2. Who or what determines the main directions of economic development?
3. Who or what shapes the cultural environment?
4. Who or what determines the contours of the material environment?
5. Do some social groups dominate decision making in all or several of these sectors?
6. Why does government do what it does?
7. What is the role of democratic institutions in these various decision-making processes?

This book is concerned with the overall impact of government activity in an environment of formal democracy and corporate capitalism. It focuses less on government institutions than on public policy and its impact on society. It seeks to understand why government does what it does with its vast resources and manpower, how it came to act in the way it does, and with what consequences it carries out its functions.

Political life also comprises values, ethics, the search for the good life; it is concerned with issues about which people feel strongly. The political analyst is invariably caught up in the issues and problems that wrack political life and that give it its energy and color. The analyst cannot stand completely aloof in scientific objectivity, but imposes personal values on his or her work. Rather than deplore this situation, which is natural and inevitable, we ought to accept it and proceed with our analysis on that basis. If we are self-conscious and aware of our values, our predispositions, and our special points of view, we can use them as standards by which to judge the worth of political processes and outcomes. I shall attempt to do that here. I shall not only *describe* the American system, but ask about its worth, its utility, and its moral standing. In addition to describing, in short, I want to *evaluate*. To evaluate, one must construct clear, precise, and consistent standards against which to judge the American system. The two standards that seem to arise naturally from descriptions of the distributions of social rewards and decision-making power are *social justice* and *democracy*. Chapter 2 will defend these choices and discuss their various meanings.

NOTES

1. Upton Sinclair, *The Jungle* (New York: Harper & Row, 1951, reprint of 1906 edition), pp. 98–99.
2. Testimony of Dr. Irving J. Selikoff before the U.S. Senate Subcommittee on Labor, May 5, 1970.
3. Testimony of Lupe Oliveras, member United Farm Workers Organizing Committee, before the U.S. House Select Subcommittee on Labor, November 21, 1969.
4. Steve Wodka, "Pesticides Since Silent Spring," in Garrett de Bell, ed., *Environmental Handbook* (New York: Ballantine, 1970), p. 85.
5. Testimony of Lacy Wright before the U.S. Senate Subcommittee on Labor, April 28, 1970.
6. Lawrence White, *Human Debris: The Injured Worker in America* (New York: Seaview/Putnam, 1983), p. 50.
7. Brief for Appellee at 33–35, *People* v. *O'Neil*, Nos. 85-1853, 85-1854, 85-1855, 85-1952, 85-1953 (App. Ct. Ill. appeal docketed July 1, 1985) (citing the medical examiner's report).
8. Timothy Egan, "Low Odds and High Perils of Logging," *The New York Times*, November 4, 1987, p. 8.
9. *The New York Times*, November 22, 1968.
10. Ibid.
11. All of the above quotes are from *The New York Times*, November 22, 1968.
12. Scholars point out that the information-gathering process in the United States is so flawed, depending almost entirely on company reports, that we can do no better than estimate the level of work-related death, injury, and disease. For a discussion of this issue, see Ray Elling, *The Struggle for Workers' Health: A Study of Six Industrialized Countries* (Farmingdale, N.Y.: Baywood Publishing, Inc., 1986), Ch. 1.
13. For these figures and how they have been estimated, see Elling, *The Struggle for Workers' Health*, Ch. 1.
14. Daniel M. Berman, *Death on the Job* (New York: Monthly Review Press, 1978). Like Elling, Berman makes the case that official statistics on the United States systematically *understate* the scale of the problem.

15. *The Yearbook of Labour Statistics, 1986* (Geneva: International Labour Office, 1987), Table 29.
16. Elling, *The Struggle for Workers' Health,* p. 22.
17. Paul Nyden, "An Internal Colony: Labor Conflict and Capitalism in Appalachian Coal," *The Insurgent Sociologist* 8 : 4 (Winter, 1979), p. 34.
18. Ben Franklin, "The Scandal of Death and Injury in the Mines," *The New York Times Magazine,* March 30, 1967, p. 122.
19. *President's Report on Occupational Safety and Health,* Commerce Department Clearing House, May 22, 1972, p. 111.
20. Governor Aretas Brooks Fleming remained on retainer to major energy companies during his entire term of office. For penetrating analyses of the economics and politics of the Appalachian region, see Harry Caudill, *Night Comes to the Cumberlands* (Boston: Little, Brown, 1962); Harry Caudill, *Theirs Be the Power: The Moguls of Eastern Kentucky* (Urbana, Ill.: University of Illinois Press, 1983); and John Gaventa, *Power and Powerlessness: Quiescence and Rebellion in an Appalachian Valley* (Urbana: University of Illinois Press, 1980).
21. Franklin, "The Scandal of Death and Injury in the Mines," p. 124.
22. Most of the safety improvement in mining during this period, according to industry observers, is attributable to the shift from deep-pit mining to above-surface strip mining.
23. *United Mine Workers Journal,* July 1–15, 1974, p. 9.
24. Harry M. Caudill, "Manslaughter in a Coal Mine," *The Nation,* April 23, 1977, p. 496.
25. Jerry DeMuth, "The Deadly Results of Coal Deregulations," *America,* January 8, 1983, pp. 8–10.
26. Most studies have, in fact, demonstrated that the costs of safety compliance are nowhere near as burdensome as business interests claim. See James Crawford, "The Dismantling of OSHA," *The Nation,* September 12, 1981, pp. 205–207.
27. Philip Simon and Kathleen Hughes, "OSHA, Industry's New Friend," *The New York Times,* September 5, 1983, p. 17.
28. Cited in White, *Human Debris,* p. 149.
29. In the social sciences this approach goes by the name of *political economy,* primarily but not solely derived from Marxist social theory (contributors to the political economy tradition also include such thinkers as Adam Smith, John Locke, David Ricardo, and John Stuart Mill). It remains to say a word about *Marxism.* To some, Marxism is a theory celebrating violent revolution, a perception reinforced by the media's tendency to label every half-baked terrorist act in the world as Marxist led or inspired. To others, Marxism is the basis of a secular state religion supporting the practices of Soviet-style regimes dominated by Marxist-Leninist parties. In these pages, Marxism is a particularly rich social theory useful as a tool for the analysis of societies in general and capitalism in particular. As with any scientific theory, its propositions and claims are open to testing and are not to be accepted or rejected as a matter of faith. For a particularly brilliant exploration of these issues, see Robert Heilbroner, *Marxism: For and Against* (New York: Norton, 1980).

2

Evaluating the American System: Justice and Democracy

The aim of this book is to help readers understand the political processes and institutions of their society; to grapple with the implications of these political phenomena for their lives; and to compare the political life of their society to that of others. Understanding social processes and institutions always involves a two-fold operation: first, a factual understanding of the principal relationships under consideration, and second, a capacity for making judgments about the ultimate worth of such relationships. Most of this text will be devoted to a detailed, factual description of the complex world of American politics and government. The purpose of this chapter is to demonstrate how one might make informed judgments about the worth of American political arrangements.

Most of the time, we tend to evaluate political, social, and economic practices carelessly, working from a base of common sense and unexamined assumptions and prejudices. Informed evaluation, on the other hand, requires a clearly articulated and consistently applied set of standards against which to compare these practices. There are, of course, many possible standards for evaluating American political life, ranging from efficiency to equity. Since we are uniting description and evaluation as two parts of the process of understanding in this text, however, we shall use the evaluative standards that most reasonably evolve out of our factual analysis.

Our first concern is with the general distribution of goods, benefits, services, and burdens in American society. The following questions immediately arise when one observes such distributions: "Is it right?" "Is it fair?" "Is it just?" These questions can be subsumed under a category customarily termed *social justice*. Our second general concern is with the distribution of decision-making power in American society. The questions that immediately suggest themselves have to do

15

with the relative balance between elites and masses in the decision process, and the relative influence of ordinary citizens versus representatives of wealth and property. Such considerations ultimately lead to the issue of *democracy*.

Is America just? Is America democratic? These two questions will be raised continually throughout the remainder of the book. The questions seem appropriate not only because of their logical connection to the factual materials we shall be examining, but because they are questions about which Americans have been deeply concerned since the founding of the Republic.

SOCIAL JUSTICE

Is America a just society? The problem we face in trying to answer this question is that no generally agreed upon definition of justice exists. Indeed, the word *justice* has been used in such a wide variety of ways that one is tempted to consider it meaningless. What lies at the heart of the confusion about justice is that all such definitions are based upon personal moral and ethical positions. In any consideration of justice, one cannot avoid making some hard moral choices; there is no neutral, scientific procedure for arriving at a universally acceptable definition. Since the term *justice* has been used so ambiguously and since people differ widely in their ethical choices, it is likely that any two people, if asked, would give different definitions. How then can we construct a standard of justice against which to measure the American system?

In fact, we cannot arrive at a single, unified definition of social justice about which all Americans might agree. It is possible, however, to identify a handful of enduring positions to which political philosophers, political practitioners, and the public have gravitated over the centuries. The following discussion examines these positions. Particular attention is paid to the assumptions made by each theory of justice, the institutional arrangements considered appropriate to each, and the expected relative inequality in benefit distribution. As you attempt to answer the question "Is America just?" by examining the factual materials that come later in this text, you should keep these various formulations of justice in mind.

Classical Conservatism and Social Justice

To avoid confusion, the conservatism I refer to in this section has little to do with what we call conservatism in the United States today, the conservatism of William F. Buckley, Milton Friedman, George Gilder, Jack Kemp, or Ronald Reagan. As strange as it may seem, the position of these individuals is, in a historical sense, a form of *liberal* theory. Historically understood, classical conservatism is a system of thought that arises primarily out of feudal and aristocratic societies, and is virtually nonexistent in the United States. Opposed to such traditional American values as progress, change, mobility, open opportunity, and equality of rights, classical conservatism poses the necessity and desirability of stability, order, harmony, social *in*equality, and leadership by a natural aristocracy.

Plato is the best-known proponent of the classical conservative position. His book *The Republic* sketches the outlines of an ideal society characterized by perfect justice, which he defines as harmony and order. Much as in the healthy human body, where each organ plays a particular and restricted function, so also in society, harmony exists when all individuals perform functions appropriate to their innate abilities. The just society is one in which such attributes can be identified in people, where people can be assigned appropriate roles and where they can be convinced to remain happily at their assigned functions.

To Plato, people have neither comparable abilities nor comparable potentialities. In his view, most people are fit only for various forms of productive labor, primarily small-scale farming. Another and smaller group of people is fit, by virtue of temperament and physical ability, for fighting and soldiering. Finally, an extremely small group, because of its intellect and philosophic training, is capable of true knowledge and is therefore fit to govern society. A just society is one in which each class of people plays its assigned function. To Plato, such an arrangement serves both the requirements of society (which must produce the means of subsistence, and be protected and governed) and the requirements of citizens, who are happiest when doing that for which they are most suited. This mode of thinking remains the basis for all forms of classical conservatism to the present day. [1]

Feudal Europe and the medieval Catholic church also held a basically conservative world view, one stressing order, loyalty, harmony, and place. The justification for such a social order was based not upon a Socratic form of reasoning, as was true for Plato, but upon natural law known through divine revelation. Despite these differences in method of deduction, Plato, the church fathers, and the feudal nobility all agreed about the static nature of human society, the fixed places of various classes of people, the harmony that is possible only through loyalty, obedience, and narrowly restricted personal initiative, and the necessity and appropriateness of governance by a naturally superior class of people.

In the late eighteenth century, English parliamentarian Edmund Burke formulated his version of classical conservative doctrine in the course of attacking the radical virus of the French Revolution. Even in its moderate stage, the French Revolution posed a series of dangers in Burke's mind, for it spread ideas of progress, change, social contract, and personal initiative. Such an upheaval could only cause anguish to a man who argued that society was not something created by a contract among people (and thus revocable by people), but was rather a holy, organic thing, created both by divine guidance and by the historical experience of the human race. A revolution that destroyed at a stroke the French *ancien régime* could only cause horror to one who conceived a naturally static society in which each class had a fixed place, and in which a natural aristocracy, because of convention, tradition, and its own ability, was alone fit to provide society with cultural, social, spiritual, and political guidance. To Burke, inequality in all things was not only inescapable, but necessary in a harmonious and just society.

The classical conservative position is sharply distinguished from the other positions we shall discuss in its frank admission of the necessity, inevitability, and desirability of inequality in all sectors of social life, from access to rights and privileges to the distribution of material benefits. Other positions assume that equality is an unarguable, axiomatic value, that unequal treatment of some members of society relative to others, while permissible, needs convincing justification.

Classical conservatism never found a comfortable home in the United States, given the absence of a feudal past with its characteristic landed aristocracy, the weakness in the early Republic of the Catholic church, and the presence of an open frontier society where status differences were difficult to sustain. This is not to say, of course, that no such classical conservative seedlings were planted in American soil—note especially John C. Calhoun and George Fitzhugh's defense of slavery—but we can say that the soil proved most inhospitable.

Classical Liberalism and Social Justice

Classical liberalism is the bedrock of American culture (as we shall see in chapter 3), and the classical liberal theory of justice is the one that is the most familiar to Americans. Classical liberalism is a way of looking at the world that is derived from the experience of early market societies and from reflections on such societies by such philosophers as Adam Smith, David Ricardo, and John Locke. The starting point for this formulation of justice is a belief in the self-regulating nature of the free market and in the naturally acquisitive, competitive character of human beings. Justice, in this view, is what happens in an ideal free market, where each individual is free to pursue his or her self-interest and to acquire property.

Rather than review all of the many varieties of liberal thought, let us turn to a particularly clear statement of the liberal theory of justice presented in Robert Nozick's *Anarchy, State and Utopia*.[2] Nozick's starting point is the claim that "individuals have rights, and there are things no person or group may do to them [without violating their rights]" (p. ix). Of all these rights, the one that stands out in importance is the right to accumulate, enjoy, and transfer property. From this premise, Nozick proceeds to construct a defense for the accumulation of unequal wealth in a just society.

To what possessions is a person entitled? Nozick's response is that a person is entitled to those things acquired through a just process. A just process of acquisition, following the lead of philosopher John Locke, is the accumulation of property holdings through the exercise of one's talents and labors in such a way that no other person is worse off by not having available that which was accumulated. Individuals have the right, after accumulating property holdings, to do with their possessions anything that does not intrude upon the province of others, including transferring those possessions to others through gifts and inheritances. To Nozick, justice is about a process, a right way of doing things and not about results. There is no a priori method to judge the justice of any final distribution of material things. The existence of significant inequalities in income, wealth, housing, health care, and so on tells us nothing about the justice or injustice of a society. The determination of justice is tied exclusively to a determination of whether individuals are *entitled* to the possessions they have under the distribution. The proper procedure to determine this is to inquire into the justice of the original acquisition of possessions and their transfer to others.

To define justice as anything other than a process, according to Nozick, cannot help but interfere with the rights of some individuals. People, in their infinite variety and complexity, will voluntarily choose to do diverse things with their possessions. Any distribution based on some value requires that some people be forcibly separated from their possessions whether it be in the name of merit, morality, equality, or some other value. Any such distribution, in Nozick's view, is not only arbitrary but unjust, because it interferes with the right of individuals to use their possessions as they see fit.

In short, a just distribution is *any* distribution that results from a just process. This just process entails a marketplace characterized by voluntary participation and free competition. Justice is, therefore, equality of rights and equality of opportunity. Justice is silent about the final form of benefit distributions. In the real world, this understanding of the concept of justice can be and has been used to justify rather severe inequalities in material conditions.

There is a great deal of evidence that the American people are strongly committed to this market-based conception of justice and see even highly unequal distributions of wealth and income in society as "just desserts." In this view, Americans are inclined to believe that people, in general and in the end, get what they deserve. They are inclined, therefore, to support governmental efforts like the Headstart Program and educational grants that concentrate on helping people compete in the job market, but to be strongly opposed to programs that redistribute resources to the "undeserving poor," who are "undeserving" by virtue of their presumed unwillingness to work and to compete.[3]

Twentieth-Century Liberalism. Nozick follows a long line of classical liberal theorists stretching from Adam Smith and John Locke to Milton Friedman and George Gilder. These theorists believe the just society to be immanent in the free operations of the marketplace. Most people who call themselves liberals in the twentieth century, however, while continuing to give primacy to the institutions of private property and the marketplace, have felt terribly uncomfortable with the severe inequalities allowed—indeed, required—by the free market position. These liberals have made various attempts to incorporate some measure of equality into liberalism. Modern liberals, among them Presidents Wilson, Roosevelt, Truman, Kennedy, and Johnson, while retaining a belief in the marketplace and in the need to protect property, have also believed that government is obliged to intervene in economic and social life in order to dampen the sharp inequalities that are a natural byproduct of the free market.[4] Government must at least minimally care for some of the wreckage wrought by its operations: poverty, unemployment, pollution, and the like. Because they believe in the primacy of private property, however, liberal political leaders have not found it possible to attack the main institution that generates inequality. While the modern liberal's heart tugs toward greater equality, the commitment to the primacy of free-enterprise market capitalism burdens him with the fact of inequality.[5]

Socialism and Social Justice

While classical conservatism celebrates inequality, and while classical liberalism allows for stark inequalities of distribution in practice, socialism has always been committed to substantial equality as a basic element of a just society. To be sure, some inequalities in the distribution of benefits and burdens have appeared in societies that call themselves socialist (though to a far lesser degree than in capitalist societies).[6] Some socialist thinkers have not even made the question of equality the first priority: Karl Marx, for instance, was more interested in the problems of class conflict and of exploitation. Yet the belief that the good society is one in which equality is the operative rule of social organization pervades the history of socialist thought.[7] Though pre- and post-Marx socialists have often sharply disagreed about the best way to make social change, the role of the vanguard party, or the proper function of the state, postrevolutionary, post-capitalist society is conceived as one composed of freely associated, equal producers who shape their group life through voluntary cooperation.[8]

The socialist position has always been that, by virtue of their common humanity, people are equal in rights, claims, and potential. To allow substantial inequality is to reject this common humanity: hence the position that the urgent needs of all must be met before satisfying the private claims of the few. To socialists, inequality represents an attack on the human essence: it denies most people the opportunity to participate fully as citizens in the political life of the community, and it denies them the right to determine the directions of their creative and productive life. From this socialist perspective, exploitation, alienation, and material inequality merge into a single problem.

To socialist thinkers, equality is one of the central standards by which both capitalist and socialist societies may be judged. In Marx's words (in *The German Ideology*), "one of the most vital principles of communism . . . is its view . . . that differences of brain, of intellectual capacity, do not imply any differences whatsoever in the nature of the stomach, and of physical needs; therefore, the false tenet . . . 'to each according to his capacity,' must be changed . . . into the tenet 'to each according to his need.'" Or more simply, socialism is only assured when distribution of all benefits and burdens follows the maxim (from *The Communist Manifesto*) "from each according to his ability; to each according to his need."

Socialists also argue that the traditional and oft-expressed claim that freedom and equality are contradictory concepts, is a false one, since inequalities in material condition block the free exercise of liberties.[9] Equality, in this view, is the precondition for the expression of human individuality. Only with an end to the exploitation of the many by the few, and the strengthening of common humanity through material, social, and political equality, will humankind have constructed the base upon which true diversity of human abilities, interests, and needs can freely develop. It is only after individuals develop their uniquely human capacities, argue socialists, that fellowship and fraternity become possible.

Social Justice as Evaluative Standard

The discussion of justice may seem to some readers a confusing trip through the philosophic bramble bushes, while to others it might appear to be an over-simplification of a most complex subject. Granted the danger of offending both sets of readers, it would probably be useful to summarize the analysis thus far. I would suggest that discussions of social justice have organized themselves around three primary nodes:

Karl Marx: the giant of the socialist tradition

☐ *Classical Conservatism:* the belief that inequality of status and condition is not only inevitable and natural, but basic to the operations of the good society. This is considered true particularly to the extent that the naturally superior are better able to lead society.

☐ *Classical Liberalism:* the belief that the just society is one in which people have equal opportunity to practice civil and political freedoms, and to pursue their self-interest in the marketplace. Inequality, while not celebrated, is interpreted as a natural byproduct of a free society. Moreover, the effort to eliminate inequality is seen as potentially dangerous to the free society itself.

☐ *Socialism:* the belief that the just society is one composed of social, political, and economic equals.

It is evident, then, that no single definition of social justice is available to us, although we have narrowed the hundreds of candidates down to three. To the question "Is America just?" we now have three clearly articulated positions from which to choose. These positions can act as standards against which to measure the real-world activities and practices of American society.

This book will demonstrate that *the United States is not a just society,* by whatever standard one chooses to use. It is certainly not surprising that the United States meets neither the classical conservative test, that being a historically archaic position never very popular in this country, nor the stringent socialist test of equality. What is surprising is the degree to which the United States fails to meet the rather minimal classical liberal tests of equality of rights, freedoms, and opportunities. Such a failure is not merely accidental, but is inherent (as we shall see in subsequent chapters) in the very economic organization of liberal society: capitalism.

DEMOCRACY

As was true for the concept of justice, it is impossible to locate a single, mutually agreed upon definition for the concept of democracy. While it might seem quite simple and uncomplicated on its face, the term *democracy* has been used in many contradictory ways. The problem with the concept is its great popularity. The word *democracy* has gained such esteem around the globe that virtually all political regimes attempt to envelop their rule in democracy's warm glow. We thus hear of *people's democracies, stockholder democracy, union democracy, pluralist democracy, interest group democracy, socialist democracy,* and so on. Confusion and ambiguity have invariably followed in the wake of this popularity. To most Americans, democracy is essentially a system of political organization in which certain rights and liberties exist. By defining democracy in this way, they miss other, perhaps richer ways of thinking about and practicing democracy. [10]

As we did with social justice, we shall examine three primary ways in which democracy has been defined. We shall attempt to demonstrate that no single democratic theory exists, and that there are competing notions, each of which implies different citizen behavior, different expectations of human capacities, and different institutional arrangements.

Direct Democracy

Most Americans associate democracy with elections, representation, and civil liberties. Yet until recent times the core meaning of democracy has been that kind of political society in which *direct, face-to-face* participation by ordinary people in their own governance is practiced. [11] In its original sense, democracy simply meant government by and for the common people. It was understood as a system of governance and a way of life in which the great mass of ordinary people acted publicly to affect the directions of collective life. One immediately thinks of the New England town meeting and the Israeli kibbutz as modern examples of this ancient form of democracy.

Central to this notion of democracy is direct, face-to-face participation in community decision making. To the Greeks, the meaning of the term *citizen* was inseparable from this notion of continuous involvement in the public life of the community. To be a passive observer, to be unconnected to the decision processes that established the overall direction of community affairs, was to be a non-

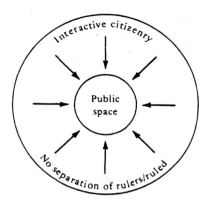

FIGURE 2.1   Direct democracy

citizen. To the Greeks, citizenship entailed not a set of *rights* and *freedoms* opposed to the interests of the community—that is, it was not a "negative" concept involving freedom from interference by others, including government (as in our Bill of Rights)—but a set of obligations and opportunities to participate in governance. One might even go further and say that, to the Greeks, people were only human to the extent that they were part of and involved in the life of human community, and to the extent that they interacted with other human beings in the public arena. It was believed that in such a public space, through public discussion, deliberation, and argument, the distance between ruler and ruled would be obliterated, as would the distance between amateur and professional politician, making for a situation of political equality and mutual respect (see Figure 2.1). [12]

Involvement in public deliberations whereby community life is directed is thus at the heart of this conception of democracy. Taking the reverse side of this democratic coin, theorists of direct participatory democracy have often defined "tyranny" not so much as the transgression of rights and freedoms by a ruler, but as the interference by the ruler in the legitimate participatory role of the citizen. As Hannah Arendt has stated:

> Tyranny . . . was a form of government in which the ruler, even though he ruled according to the laws of the realm, had monopolized for himself the right of action, banished the citizens from the public realm into the privacy of their households, and demanded of them that they mind their own, private business. Tyranny, in other words, deprived the public of happiness, though not necessarily of private well-being, while a republic granted to every citizen the right to become "a participator in the government of affairs," the right to be seen in action. [13]

The conception of democracy as "direct," "face-to-face," and "participatory" (that is, not mediated through other persons or institutions) represents an important deviation from historic conceptions of the proper organization and operation of the political community. Social and political thought through the ages has tended toward autocratic, aristocratic, or elitist notions of governance. To most political practitioners and thinkers, governance was considered to be a difficult art requiring the greatest sophistication, intelligence, character, and training. It was not something to be left to the whims and devices of ordinary people. Whether one finally settled on a superior social class, a king, a philosopher, or a religious elect as the proper ruler, most political philosophers and practitioners imposed formidable barriers to the participation of the common person in government.

When seen against centuries of such thinking, it is clear that democratic theory, defined as self-governance by ordinary people, represented an important departure. Most of the thinkers acknowledged today as the progenitors of democracy believed that everyone has deliberative and moral potential; that, given the proper education and environment, ordinary people could be responsible and reflective. At the heart of classical democratic theory is this faith in the capacity of ordinary human beings to govern themselves wisely.

> The foundation of democracy is faith in the capacities of human nature; faith in human intelligence and in the power of pooled and cooperative experience. It is not belief that these things are complete but that if given a show they will grow and be able to generate progressively the knowledge and wisdom needed to guide collective action. [14]

The conception of democracy as direct and face-to-face has never enjoyed much popularity in the United States, perhaps because of the sheer size and social complexity of a continental nation. The one great exception is the New Left student movement of the sixties, inspired by the struggle of black Americans for civil rights and destined to shape the language and style of the anti–Vietnam War movement. The commitment of the New Left to a more direct form of democracy is best articulated in the famous *Port Huron Statement* of the Students for a Democratic Society (more commonly known as SDS):

> Americans are in withdrawal from public life, from any collective effort at directing their own affairs. Some regard this national doldrums as a sign of healthy approval of the established order. . . . Still others think that the national quietude is a necessary consequence of the need for elites to solve complex and specialized problems of modern industrial society. . . . Others, finally, shrug knowingly and announce that full democracy has never existed anywhere in the past. . . .
> The very isolation of the individual from power and community and ability to aspire means the rise of a democracy without publics. With the great mass of people structurally remote and psychologically hesitant with respect to democratic institutions, those institutions themselves attenuate and become, in the fashion of a vicious circle, progressively less accessible to those few who aspire to serious participation in social affairs. . . .
> As a social system we seek the establishment of a participatory democracy, governed by two central aims: that the individual share in those social decisions determining the quality and direction of his life; that society be organized to encourage independence in men and provide the means for their common participation. [15]

Liberal-Representative Democracy

Central to direct democracy is the notion that government and the governed are identical, that no distance exists between ruler and ruled; or, more basically, that within the boundaries of the political community, ruler and ruled are identical: *citizens*. In a principal-competing model of democracy, *representative democracy*, government and the governed are separate and distinct, and politics becomes a process not of deliberation but of forging instruments by which citizens may exercise some control over and protection against government leaders (see Figure 2.2). In this conception, the people rule indirectly, through representatives authorized to make policy decisions in the name of those who elected them. While citizen participation remains an important constituent element, it is limited to the periodic election of persons who act as representatives, and to the occasional transmission of instructions to them.

Why representative democracy rather than the inherently more appealing "direct" variety? Why substitute an essentially two-step process of participation for the more unitary one? Most central to these questions, in the view of political scientist Robert Dahl, are problems of size and time.[16] First, there is an upper limit to the size of a group that can meet and deliberate face to face. Once a certain maximum size is surpassed, it is not feasible to allow everyone to express a view or opinion about whatever matter is under consideration. Second, a general meeting of the political community cannot be in continuous session, since all members of that community have other concerns to which they must attend, including those of family and livelihood.

While representative democracy can compensate for certain inherent problems in the "direct," participatory variant, it is itself prone to serious difficulties relating to the distance between citizen, representative, and government. First, to reiterate a point already made, participation in such a system is only intermittent, involving the election of representatives and the occasional conveyance of demands or expressions of concern to those representatives. Such a limited involvement potentially destroys the capacity of self-governance to be educative

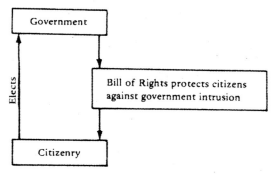

FIGURE 2.2   Liberal-representative democracy

Indirect democracy: voting for representatives

and broadening in its effect. Second, representative democratic systems have a strong tendency to create a professional political class—a group of people who make life as a representative a full-time occupation, while the ordinary citizen assumes amateur status. The possibility that this professional class will go its own way, evolving policy in directions inconsistent with popular desires, is obvious. Finally, as the distance between government and governed becomes pronounced, a central concern of the governed becomes that of defining and protecting a private space into which a potentially threatening government might intrude unless limited and constrained. It is with respect to this recurrent problem that questions of rights and liberties come center stage, and the conception of active self-governance recedes to the wings. The sacred core of political life becomes the protection of the people against government interference with the exercise of their liberties. For most Americans, the essence of democracy has come to mean a system in which individual freedoms exist (freedoms of speech, association, religion, and so on); in which certain judicial rights are available (such as due process of law, trial by jury, freedom from self-incrimination); and in which people have the right to freely elect representatives.

Pluralist Democracy

Modern political science has formulated yet another conception of democracy: pluralism, or pluralist democracy. This formulation, rooted in the writings of James Madison (especially in his justly famous #10 of *The Federalist Papers*) and given modern form by political scientists Robert Dahl, Charles Lindblom, and David Truman (among others) in the 1950s and 1960s, represents a rejection of direct, participatory democracy and an extension of representative democracy. Participatory democracy (see Figure 2.3) is rejected because of its purported "utopian" qualities, that is to say, the impossibility of its functioning in a modern, populous, industrial society. Representative democracy is seen in the pluralist view as correct yet limited in the sense that it fails to capture the richness and complexity of the functioning modern democracies like the United States.[17]

Pluralism starts from two basic assumptions:

1. *That citizens of the United States do not measure up to the standards set by theorists of democracy.* Theorists of direct democracy, such as J. S. Mill and Rousseau, talked about a democratic citizen who was essentially *rational, informed,* and *interested* in political life. Such a description, say the pluralists, sets much too great a demand on the limited capacity of ordinary people. This is demonstrated by social science research that clearly shows that most Americans are uninformed about politics and are neither overly interested nor particularly sophisticated about political events.

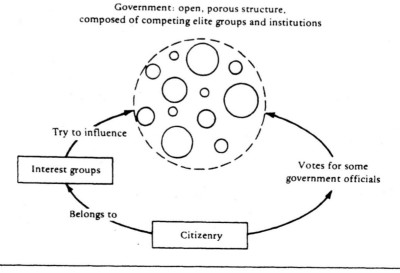

FIGURE 2.3   Pluralist democracy

2. *That the system works.* Pluralists argue that while the distance between pluralism and the classical, participatory conception is enormous, the American system works, and often with distinction. It provides not only for the peaceful transfer of power between ruling groups, but for a method whereby the voices of all groups with interests in government policy are heard and considered.

In juxtaposing research evidence about the shortcomings of American citizens with their own belief in the democratic character of the United States, pluralist theorists go on to claim that it is the prevailing theory of democracy that is wrong, not the operating system, and that democratic theory must, as a result, be reformulated. What does this theory look like?

The Functional Necessity of Apathy. Since most citizens are uninformed, uninterested, and often irrational in political areas, it is best that they should remain apathetic, especially since the system works so well. Indeed, since the system works the way it does without widespread popular involvement, it must follow that there is something necessary or functional about apathy.

Apathy is not evenly distributed through the population, but is correlated very strongly with the stratification system. Those near the top social stratum are more likely to be participants than those near the bottom. We should be thankful for this, because it is primarily among the masses that we find, according to sociologist Seymour Martin Lipset, extremist-millennial religious movements (implying rigid fundamentalism and dogmatism), irrationality and prejudice, insecurity and instability, simplistic views and personal concerns, and anti-intellectualism and authoritarianism.

In light of this picture of the uninvolved yet potentially dangerous masses, we should not regret noninvolvement (as do "get out the vote" groups), but heave a sigh of relief that things are as they are. If this untapped pool were mobilized, it would be a source of extreme danger and instability for the democratic system of the United States, according to this view.

If we cannot depend on the mass population for support of democratic principles and practice, to whom can we turn? How does the system continue to operate as well as it does?

Democracy and Elites. In contrast to Jefferson's profound skepticism about elites, pluralist theorists have come to believe that the very survival of democratic systems depends on elites, who are the repository for democratic values. Thus, political scientist V. O. Key, after reviewing evidence from public opinion studies that seemingly demonstrates that persons from the upper reaches of society are more likely than those from the lower to hold to democratic norms (tolerance, belief in free speech, openness to public opinion, playing by the rules, rejection of "total politics," and so on), argues that "*the critical element for the health of a democratic order consists in the beliefs, standards, and competence of those who constitute the influentials, the opinion-leaders, the political activists in the order.*"[18]

This is closely related to the concept of functional apathy. Since elites are supportive of a democratic system, and since the masses have serious antidemocratic tendencies, it is fortunate that politics is primarily the domain of elites. This phenomenon has been praised as the *division of political labor*, allowing elites the elbow room they need for action in a world of great complexity and danger. Interference from ordinary citizens brings emotionalism, irrationality, and delay into the deliberations of policy makers.

It is not at all apparent how a system based on elite policy making and mass noninvolvement can legitimately be called democracy. How do pluralists deal with this thorny problem? They do so by means of two methods for transmitting mass wants, aspirations, and demands to government officials: elite competition and interest groups.

Elite Competition. We have seen that those who are economically, socially, and educationally "better off" are the major actors in politics. It is the less well off who make up the bulk of the apathetic. We have also heard the claim that such a state of affairs is fortunate, given the democratic proclivities of the elites and the antidemocratic proclivities of the masses. *What keeps this division of labor from evolving into a rigid oligarchy is the intense competition among groups of elites.* The elite stratum is united only on the "rules of the game"; beyond that, it is riven by deep divisions of interest and inclination. *Moreover, it is primarily by means of this competition that elites remain open and responsive to pressure from the mass public.* Thus, elite competition, whether taking place through elections or through interest group conflict and bargaining, serves democratic values. As Dahl says, "Democratic theory is concerned with processes by which ordinary citizens exert a relatively high degree of control over leaders." [19] Perhaps the purest statement of the relationship between elite competition and the body of citizens was made by Joseph Schumpeter in *Capitalism, Socialism and Democracy*. His claim is that the democratic process involves nothing more than a method by which potential leaders compete for the vote, and where the role of the citizen is to help produce a government, to choose leaders, and then to withdraw from participation. Government, in a nice reversal of Lincoln, is government not *by* the people but one occasionally *approved* or pressured *by* the people.

Interest Groups. Pluralist theorists understand American society to be composed of a complex set of groups, each with a distinct set of interests and goals. Pluralists also assume that most Americans belong to a variety of groups and seek through such groups, ranging from the American Medical Association to the NAACP and the American Automobile Association, to advance their own interests and aspirations. It is the competition and bargaining among and between these many groups that is the essence of the political process. The role of government, in the pluralist view, is that of umpire (setting and enforcing the "rules of the game") and scorekeeper. Government is the scorekeeper in the sense that the public policies it produces (laws, regulations, and so on) are simply the formal outcomes of the various contests between and the bargains struck among the many interest groups in American society.

This interest group system, in the pluralist view, is democratic in two fundamental ways. First, groups are so easy to form that ordinary Americans may choose to create one whenever they feel the need to advance their interests and aspirations in the political process. Second, government in the United States is so permeable and accessible—through elections, the courts, lobbying, and the like—that any and all groups in society can have their views heard and considered at some point in the policy-making process. To the pluralists, while democracy is quite indirect in this conception, it is truer to the ways in which actual democracies work in places like the United States and Great Britain.

Democracy as Evaluative Standard

In attempting to answer the question "Is America democratic?" we now have available three distinct models of democracy that can be used to evaluate the everyday operations of the American system. Each one asks us to look at different aspects of that system. The participatory model compels us to look at the civic lives of Americans, and to ask whether they are active participants in the processes by which public policies are decided. Liberal-representative democracy compels us to look at the state of civil liberties in the United States, the availability of juridical protection of rights, and the quality of the relationship between elected representatives and the electorate. Pluralism asks us to look at elites in American society with an eye toward determining the extent to which they are competitive, open, and responsive to mass aspirations, and at the vitality and competitiveness of the interest group system. I shall take the perhaps surprising position in this book that *the United States does not fulfill the expectations of any of the democratic models*, though, to be sure, it comes closer to fitting some (liberal-representative) than others (participatory). You are urged, of course, to reach your own conclusions, comparing the factual materials to the models in the pages that follow.

CONCLUDING REMARKS

This chapter has developed several ways to evaluate the American system, to answer the questions "Is America just?" and "Is America democratic?" There are, to be sure, any number of other ways to evaluate the American system. Nevertheless, *social justice* and *democracy* remain the most important standards of evaluation in this book, not only because of their obvious connections to the descriptive materials we will encounter in the chapters that follow, but also because of the great concern for social justice and democracy that Americans have demonstrated throughout their history.

This discussion of the forms of justice and democracy should serve other important functions as well. It should demonstrate that most political language is value-laden and imprecise (when people use words such as *justice, democracy, community,* and *freedom,* one ought to ask what is meant by them); that modern social science comes perilously close to traditional conservative and aristocratic views without openly admitting so; and most importantly, that other possibilities exist in the world, that alternative forms of social and political organization are available, and that political systems are open to and capable of change. Finally, the discussions of justice and democracy should have demonstrated to you the necessity of stepping outside the boundaries of your own system to make evaluations and to develop standards of judgment independent of particular systems.

NOTES

1. Plato, however, unlike most conservative thinkers, did not equate the right to rule with the right to hold disproportionate wealth.

2. Robert Nozick, *Anarchy, State and Utopia* (New York: Basic Books, 1974).

3. See Herbert McClosky and John Zaller, *The American Ethos: Public Attitudes toward Capitalism and Democracy* (Cambridge: Harvard University Press, 1984); and Robert Lane, "Market Justice and Political Justice," *American Political Science Review* 80 : 2 (June 1986), pp. 383–402.

4. For a discussion of twentieth-century government policy and its connection to liberal reform, see Edward S. Greenberg, *Capitalism and the American Political Ideal* (Armonk, N.Y.: M. E. Sharpe, 1985); Jeff Lustig, *Corporate Liberalism* (Berkeley: University of California Press, 1982); and Alan Wolfe, *The Limits of Legitimacy* (New York: Free Press, 1977).

5. The processes by which property generates inequality will be extensively examined in later chapters. For a provocative attempt to tie liberalism to equality, see John Rawls, *A Theory of Justice* (Cambridge, Mass.: Harvard University Press, 1971).

6. For a comparison between capitalist and socialist inequalities, see Branko Horvat, *The Political Economy of Socialism* (Armonk, N.Y.: M. E. Sharpe, 1982), and Frank Parkin, *Class Inequality and Political Order* (New York: Praeger, 1971); also see Branko Horvat, "Welfare of the Common Man in Various Countries," *World Development* 2 : 7 (July 1974); and Jay Mandle, "Basic Needs and Economic Systems," *Review of Social Economics* 38 : 2 (October 1980), pp. 179–189.

7. I shall argue in the last chapter that presently existing socialist societies are not really socialist.

8. R. H. Tawney poses the appropriate response to those who oppose equality on practical grounds: "To say that since men can never have complete equality they should not try to do it, is like using the impossibility of absolute cleanliness as a pretext for rolling in a manure heap." From R. H. Tawney, *Equality* (London: Allen and Unwin, 1952), p. 134.

9. In this regard, see Kai Nielsen, *Equality and Liberty: A Defense of Radical Equalitarianism* (Totowa, N.J.: Rowman and Allanheld, 1984).

10. For a brilliant discussion of the many meanings of democracy, see C. B. MacPherson, *The Real World of Democracy* (Oxford: Clarendon Press, 1965). Also see Samuel Bowles and Herbert Gintis, *Democracy and Capitalism* (New York: Basic Books, 1986).

11. This form is called "unitary democracy" by Jane Mansbridge in her book *Beyond Adversary Democracy* (New York: Basic Books, 1980).

12. It is important to add that the Greeks held to a narrowly construed concept of the eligibility pool. Slaves and women, for instance, were not admitted to citizenship.

13. Hannah Arendt, *On Revolution* (New York: Viking Press, 1965), p. 127.

14. John Dewey, *The Public and Its Problems* (New York: Holt, 1927), p. 211.

15. For a brilliant analysis of the history and meaning of SDS, see James Miller, *Democracy Is in the Streets* (New York: Simon & Schuster, 1987).

16. Robert Dahl, *After the Revolution* (New Haven: Yale University Press, 1970).

17. The following discussion of pluralism is based upon a synthesis of the major works on this topic. While the synthesis may not be perfectly representative of any single work, my hope is that the general description I present is true to the basic intent of each. The seminal works on pluralism are the following: Bernard Berelson, "Democratic Theory and Public Opinion," *Public Opinion Quarterly* 16 (Fall, 1952), pp. 313–330; Bernard Berelson, Paul Lazarsfeld,

and William McPhee, *Voting* (Chicago: University of Chicago Press, 1954); Robert Dahl, *A Preface to Democratic Theory* (Chicago: University of Chicago Press, 1956); Robert Dahl, *Who Governs* (New Haven: Yale University Press, 1961); Robert Dahl and Charles E. Lindblom, *Politics, Economics and Welfare* (New York: Harper & Row, 1963); V. O. Key, *Public Opinion and American Democracy* (New York: Knopf, 1961); Seymour Martin Lipset, *Political Man* (New York: Doubleday, 1963); Giovanni Sartori, *Democratic Theory* (Detroit: Wayne State University Press, 1962); and Joseph A. Schumpeter, *Capitalism, Socialism and Democracy* (New York: Harper & Row, 1950). For some fascinating second thoughts about the nature of pluralism, see Charles Lindblom, *Politics and Markets* (New York: Basic Books, 1977), and Robert Dahl, *Dilemmas of Pluralist Democracy* (New Haven: Yale University Press, 1982).
18. Key, *Public Opinion and American Democracy*, p. 537.
19. Dahl, *A Preface to Democratic Theory*, p. 3.

SUGGESTIONS FOR FURTHER READING

Samuel Bowles and Herbert Gintis. DEMOCRACY AND CAPITALISM: PROPERTY, COMMUNITY, AND THE CONTRADICTIONS OF MODERN SOCIAL THOUGHT. *New York: Basic Books, 1986.* Explores the complex interrelationships of capitalism, democracy, and justice.

Robert A. Dahl. A PREFACE TO DEMOCRATIC THEORY. *Chicago: University of Chicago Press, 1956.* A concise statement of the pluralist theory of democracy.

Charles Lindblom. POLITICS AND MARKETS. *New York: Basic Books, 1977.* A stimulating reexamination of pluralist democracy with particular emphasis on the incompatibility of the giant corporation and genuine democratic politics.

Robert McClosky and John Zaller. THE AMERICAN ETHOS: PUBLIC ATTITUDES TOWARD CAPITALISM AND DEMOCRACY. *Cambridge, Mass.: Harvard University Press, 1984.* A careful look at the attitudes of elites and the mass public concerning capitalism and democracy, with some surprising conclusions.

C. B. MacPherson. A REAL WORLD OF DEMOCRACY. *Oxford: Clarendon Press, 1965.* A stimulating tour of the several meanings of democracy.

Jane Mansbridge. BEYOND ADVERSARY DEMOCRACY. *New York: Basic Books, 1980.* A highly influential empirical study of the tension in organizations between unitary and adversary democracy.

John Stuart Mill. ON REPRESENTATIVE GOVERNMENT. *London: Everyman edition, 1910.* The classic formulation and defense of representative democracy.

James Miller. DEMOCRACY IS IN THE STREETS. *New York: Simon & Schuster, 1987.* A history of SDS that takes the organization's debates about democracy seriously.

Robert Nozick. ANARCHY, STATE AND UTOPIA. *New York: Basic Books, 1974.* Award-winning exposition of the classical liberal position on distributive justice.

Carole Pateman. PARTICIPATION AND DEMOCRATIC THEORY. *London: Cambridge University Press, 1970.* A careful analysis of the contending democratic traditions and a spirited defense of the participatory form.

John Rawls. A THEORY OF JUSTICE. *Cambridge, Mass.: Harvard University Press, 1971.* A widely discussed philosophic attempt to infuse the liberal theory of justice with equality.

R. H. Tawney. EQUALITY. *London: Allen and Unwin, 1952.* A classic statement of the socialist commitment to equality.

Part

II

The Context
and Basis of
American Politics

This section of the book argues that to understand American life in general and American political life in particular one must first understand the nature of capitalist society—its main cultural ideas, its legal norms and structures, its forms of economic organization, and its characteristic social structures.

3

The Cultural Milieu: America as a Liberal Society

Every stable society is tied together and sustained by widely disseminated sets of ideas about what is right and proper in political, economic, and social life. The United States is no exception to this general rule, for it is shaped and significantly directed by an elaborate and coherent system generally labeled *liberalism*. One cannot possibly understand American politics without first coming to grips with liberalism, for its ideas, values, and assumptions pervade every nook and cranny of our society and leave their mark on virtually every social, economic, and political decision we make individually or collectively. Liberalism is, in the words of one scholar, "*the* American ideology."[1] To another writer, liberalism is "the whole of [American] history."[2] From the viewpoint of eminent historian Louis Hartz, America has always been "a liberal civilization."[3] By *liberalism,* these writers refer to a philosophy in which notions of individualism, private property, the self-regulating market, and limited government hold center stage. An understanding of liberalism is vital in any effort to understand the American system; to a great extent, it is the basis for our major ideas about politics, about economic life, and, ultimately, about ourselves. Liberalism has no serious rival as a system of ideas in America.

Liberalism, like many other concepts used in this book, is not unambiguous in meaning. The ideas that together comprise liberalism are so familiar and pervasive, so much a part of our lives, that they seem obvious, commonsensical, even universal in their applicability. They have become the unexamined and unquestioned premises of the American people; since they are so familiar, we rarely think carefully about them, or, more important, about how commitment to such values affects our lives.

There is also the persistent problem of ambiguous terminology. Both modern liberals (stretching from President Franklin Delano Roosevelt to Senator Ted

36

Kennedy) *and* modern conservatives (stretching from Senators Robert Taft and Barry Goldwater to Ronald Reagan and columnist William F. Buckley) are liberal in the traditional sense of that term. Modern liberals and modern conservatives are but two strains within the general classical liberal tradition (see Figure 3.1). While members of these two modern strains of the liberal tradition are constantly bickering about the proper scale of government activity and responsibility, they jointly hold to the values of private property, the market, and individualism. Modern conservatives do not, for instance, call for reconstructing American life around the traditional European feudal model of conservatism (a society organized around the values of hierarchy, order, status, religion, duty, service, and the like, discussed in chapter 2). Nor do modern liberals propose eliminating market capitalism. While disagreeing about how to accomplish the traditional ends of liberalism, both are united in their common commitment to such ends.

WHAT IS LIBERALISM?

The above introduction has attempted to give the reader some notion of the centrality of liberal culture to American life, and to clear up some of the ambiguity attached to the term *liberalism*. We now examine more closely the component elements of liberal culture.

Competitive Individualism

At the heart of liberal culture is a belief that people are basically self-interested and competitive. Throughout our history, scholars, writers, and travelers to the United States have been struck by the tenacity of the competitive individualism found here. Alexis de Tocqueville, the brilliant French observer of the early republic, once described how Americans thought of themselves:

> They owe nothing to any man, they expect nothing from any man; they acquire the habit of always considering themselves as standing alone, and they are apt to imagine that their whole destiny is in their own hands.[4]

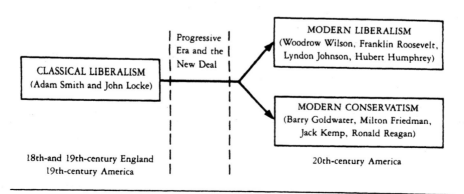

FIGURE 3.1   Modern liberalism and conservatism

De Tocqueville's short description rings true; it is entirely familiar to us. The cultural makeup of the average American (whoever that elusive creature might be) includes a belief that people are meant to stand on their own two feet; that other people owe them nothing; that they, in turn, owe nothing to others. (This standard refrain is heard in a variety of contexts, but never more clearly than in the recurrent complaints about people on welfare.) It is of more than passing interest to note that the archetypical American hero has always been the "loner," whether encountered in the traditional Western myth (Gary Cooper in *High Noon* or John Wayne in any number of films), as a private eye (Bogart in *The Maltese Falcon*), as the tough but incorruptible cop (Clint Eastwood), as the vigilante (Charles Bronson), or as the avenger (Rambo). The attitude of the lone hero is nicely captured in the following comment made by Humphrey Bogart's character to Ingrid Bergman's in the American film classic *Casablanca:* "Where I'm going, you can't follow; what I've got to do, you can't be any part of."

Closely tied to this image of the individual standing alone is the common belief that people are naturally competitive, that they are always striving to better themselves in relation to others. Their aim is to not only keep up with the Joneses, but to pass them by. An abundance of popular nonfiction literature in America has always conveyed this theme. In recent years, *The New York Times* "best seller" list has featured such titles as *Power and How to Get It, Looking Out for Number 1, Dress for Success,* and *Winning Through Intimidation,* as well as other, similar manuals of competitive advancement. The most popular autobiographies of the 1980s all celebrated making it to the top from humble beginnings: *Iaccoca, Yeager,* and *His Way* (Sinatra). Horatio Alger and Dale Carnegie, while outfitted in various forms of dress to suit the times, are always there to remind Americans of their basic nature.

Through the ages, many philosophers have contributed to this conception of human nature, with Thomas Hobbes and John Locke foremost among them. To Hobbes, in particular, man is an aggressive, competitive, ever-striving being, moved by the compulsion to fill his unlimited appetites, engaged in an ongoing "war of all against all":

> I put for a general inclination of all mankind, a perpetual and restless desire of power after power, that ceaseth only in death. And the cause of this, is not always that a man hopes for a more intensive delight, than he has already attained to; or that he cannot be content with a more moderate power: but because he cannot assure the power and means to live well, which he hath present, without the acquisition of more.[5]

The Right to Private Property

Another important element in the classical liberal belief system is the idea that human beings have a natural right to accumulate, enjoy, and transfer private property. It is mainly to seventeenth-century philosopher John Locke that we owe most of our present ideas on the subject. Locke argued that while God gave the earth and its resources to humankind in common (to be enjoyed by all), he also gave human beings a set of capacities like industry (the willingness to work hard) and creativity, which they had a right and obligation to exercise, and by so doing

John Locke: philosopher of private property and limited government

they transformed the commons into private property. Individuals, that is to say, by mixing their labor with the naturally occurring abundance of the earth (the land, forests, rivers, and so on), were justified in taking the products of that effort for their own as private property. In so doing, they not only did no harm to others, for there remained enough left for others, but increased the overall wealth and well-being of society. However, it is also the case that since people always bring different abilities and inclinations to labor to this encounter with nature, private property taken out of the commons will always be disproportionately distributed. Inevitably, some people will end up with more property than others. Out of the commons, out of the land and its resources held equally by all, naturally and through no act of coercion or theft, comes the unequal ownership of private property.

To Locke, as well as to many of his contemporaries, the right to accumulate private property and to freely enjoy the fruits of one's labor was an inalienable right, derived from God's natural law. This linkage of unequal possession of private property to natural law is crucial, for it conferred a sacred quality to the ordinary business activities of the new class of traders and merchants of Locke's time (late seventeenth-century England), who were beginning to build vast fortunes. Property rights, being sacred and natural, become fundamental to all other rights, or, more accurately, they come before other rights. According to

Locke, individuals have an inviolable right to appropriate whatever they can through their labor, and this right takes precedence over the claims of society or government. Individuals require the consent of no institution or person to carry out their acts of acquisition or to enjoy what they manage to accumulate. Property rights are fundamental, according to Locke, because such rights are inseparable from what it means to be a human being.

It follows that if property rights precede all other claims, including those of society in general, then no other person is justified in taking away any property legally acquired through one's own labor. In fact, Locke argues, it is to prevent just such an occurrence that people voluntarily come together and agree to form governments:

> The great and chief end of Men's uniting into Commonwealths, and putting themselves under government, is the Preservation of their Property.[6]

Limited Government

Derived mainly from Locke, deeply imbedded in liberal culture, and made concrete in the U.S. Constitution is the important idea that governments must remain limited in their responsibilities. Notice that in Locke the purposes of government are strictly limited to the protection of natural rights—and in particular, the set of rights connected to the acquisition, enjoyment, and transfer of private property. Under the original agreement by which it was instituted, government has no mandate to go beyond the protection of rights, for to do so would inevitably infringe upon the basic rights of some persons. If, in fact, governments do trespass these bounds, people have the right to dissolve their original compact and to form a new government. Our own Declaration of Independence, with its substance drawn almost directly from Locke, expresses this sentiment in words very familiar to Americans:

> We hold these truths to be self-evident, that all men are created equal, that they are endowed by their Creator with certain unalienable Rights, that among these are Life, Liberty and the pursuit of Happiness.[7] That to secure these rights, Governments are instituted among Men, deriving their just powers from the consent of the governed. . . . That whenever any Form of Government becomes destructive of these ends, it is the Right of the People to alter or to abolish it, and to institute new Government, laying its foundation on such principles and organizing its powers in such form, as to them shall seem most likely to effect their Safety and Happiness.

The notion of limited government is vital to the American political culture. Even while government in the United States grew vast, active, and interventionist during the twentieth century, political leaders felt duty-bound to pay homage to the liberal tradition by claiming that they had been forced by circumstances to institute some program, or that the latest government measure was only temporary. It has always been safe, and has today become mandatory, for a candidate to campaign against "big government." In recent times, the idea of limited government may be seen in various antitax referenda (like California's famous Proposition 13), the Gramm-Rudman federal budget law, and the movement to call a constitutional convention to pass a balanced budget amendment.

Deep slashes in personal and corporate income taxes and in domestic spending programs during the Reagan years (supported by most Democrats in Congress) made this commonly articulated sentiment the very centerpiece of public policy in the United States.

Since government is limited in purpose—namely, to protect property—how is it that economic and social life are able to function? How is it that economic and social life do not degenerate into the basest sort of anarchism?

The Free Market

If left alone to operate in its natural fashion, it is argued, the market acts as the main coordinating mechanism of social, economic, and political life. It is mainly to Adam Smith that we owe this insight, though it has been a standard part of the intellectual equipment of all classical liberal thinkers since the seventeenth century. Smith proposed the existence of a natural law of economic life by which the social good is served only when individuals are free to pursue their own interest in the marketplace. The breakthrough made by Smith was twofold. First, if market relations are considered part of natural law, then any government intervention in economic life constitutes interference with nature itself. In this sense, Smith was also an important contributor to ideas about limited government. Second, he linked individual selfishness to the general advance and betterment of society,

Adam Smith: the apostle of the free market

thereby reversing the entire history of values, at a stroke rendering selfishness not only palatable, but admirable.

> [Each person] is led by an invisible hand to promote an end [the common good] which was not part of his intention.[8]

The link between individual greed and social good—the instrument of the "invisible hand"—is the market mechanism.

Americans have generally believed in the naturalness, efficiency, and utility of the market mechanism, both for the individual and for society.[9] In economic life, the market is seen as a place where scarce goods and services are allocated in the best possible fashion, where goods are produced that people will want to buy at prices they are willing to pay. The market is also seen as a place where people test their skills, their abilities, and their mettle against others. Through the competitive struggle, society is well served, for such a struggle produces better people (toughened, hardened, tested) and better products. It has been traditional American belief, for instance, that interference with the market mechanism produces both inefficiencies (think of the never-ending jokes about the Postal Service) and people of deficient and warped character (people "on the dole," "welfare chiselers," and so on).

THE SOCIAL RAMIFICATIONS OF LIBERALISM

Americans are immersed in liberal culture, in a set of ideas, values, and assumptions that seem natural and inevitable, the very pinnacle of common sense. The ideas derived from classical liberalism form the milieu, the very growth medium within which all Americans find themselves. As such, it largely determines how Americans think about themselves, about other persons, and about the society around them. Liberal culture translates into the concrete, everyday life of the American people. In so doing, it takes on a variety of observable forms.

a. "Making It." Take, for instance, the place of "success" in American life. Observers of the American character, going as far back as de Tocqueville in the 1830s, have noted the primacy and tenacity of the "success ethic"—the belief in "getting ahead," "making it," striving, achieving. The "self-made man," the Horatio Alger character, is in fact a peculiarly American hero, and his myth is remarkably appealing to many, who are inspired to revise their own history in his image. Among the wealthy in America one often hears the plaint that they have earned their position through hard work, intelligence, skill, daring, and so on, and that nothing was handed to them on a "silver platter." Whether such talk is self-delusion or mere camouflage is beside the point. The power of classical liberal culture requires that the wealthy make such protestations.

b. Materialism. Observers have also noted the strong emphasis on materialism in American life. This is a natural outgrowth of the individual success ethic, for how else is one to measure one's worth relative to others? Money especially is the measure and symbol of success. This emphasis on materialism was particularly strong during the Reagan years—at least until the stock market collapse on "black Monday," October 19, 1987—with the media celebration of "go, go" investment bankers, corporate raiders, and futures traders, and the popularity of television shows like "Dynasty" and "Lifestyles of the Rich and Famous.".

The self-made individual in a success-oriented society has no other standard except money and the visible things that money buys by which to measure success. Consider the relationship between money and success in the life of Richard Nixon, for example. Garry Wills, in his stimulating examination of Nixon and of liberalism, *Nixon Agonistes,* points out:

> He had risen, politically, from the dead. And he had done it by the route these men respected—by making money. Nixon had been a candidate before . . . but only after his 1962 defeat did he become a wealthy man. . . . Only when he became a Wall Street lawyer, with $200,000 a year from his practice, and with Bebe Rebozo to help him invest in Florida land, could he look his fellow Republicans straight in the eye at last. A campaign coordinator who worked with Nixon through the years put it this way: "Dick could not have made it to first base in 1968 without a substantial personal income. Republicans, especially those who finance the party, respect only one thing, success, and they have only one way of measuring success, money. Dick never had any money before now. He could not talk to these people as an equal, even when he was Vice-President. The thing that would have killed him with them was any suspicion that he simply needed a job. Now they knew he'd be giving up a damn good job, and good money." [10]

c. Privatism and Isolation. Others have pointed out the peculiar loneliness of liberal culture and the market society, arguing that a society which stresses aggressive, individualistic competition is likely to be deficient in fellowship and community. Philip Slater argues that liberal society is essentially a frantic place, a Hobbesian world where the success of one race is challenged almost immediately by the next race, and where the natural human longing for fellowship is frustrated by the need to prevail over one's competitors:

> It is easy to produce examples of the many ways in which Americans attempt to minimize, circumvent, or deny the interdependence upon which all human societies are based. . . . An enormous technology seems to have set itself the task of making it unnecessary for one human being ever to ask anything of another in the course of going about his daily business. Even within the family Americans are unique in their feeling that each member should have a separate room, and even a separate telephone, television, and car, when economically possible. We seek more and more privacy, and feel more and more alienated and lonely when we get it. [11]

To make matters worse, there is a tendency in a society governed by classical liberal ideas to deal with alienation and loneliness in radically individualistic ways that run the gamut from organizations like est, Lifeforce, Scientology, and Esalen; to popular books like *How to Be Your Own Best Friend, Fit for Life,* and *One Minute for Myself;* to magazines like *Self* and *Psychology Today.* All of these privatized efforts to "get in touch with yourself" simply further the processes of isolation and increase the market for additional "self-help" remedies. Is it any wonder that the United States suffers the highest combined rates of alcoholism, drug use, suicide, and interpersonal violence in the world?

d. Hostility to Public Initiatives. Many years ago, the eminent economist John Kenneth Galbraith pointed out that we are a society in which there exists great private wealth and public squalor. By this he meant to suggest that Americans prefer private accumulation and enjoyment of wealth for individuals rather than a system that provides a broad range of quality public services for its citizens. In this, the United States is very different from even other developed capitalist nations, where citizens and political leaders believe that extensive and high-quality public services in the areas of mass transit, health care, housing, and education are part and parcel of the good society. In the United States, because of the pervasiveness of liberal culture, citizens and political leaders almost always prefer private consumption over public provision, and private over public initiative.[12]

e. Hostility to Ways of Life Outside the Liberal Consensus. As one might suspect, a culture that strongly believes in self-reliance, aggressiveness, and competition is unlikely to be friendly to those social groups that profess and live by other values, or that fail to live up to the expected standards. Several scholars have pointed out that social groups that live cooperatively and communally, either because they stand as living rejections of the dominant culture or because of the envy that such a "childlike," "pristine" existence seems to evoke, have been dealt with quite harshly by other Americans. The case of Native Americans is the most notable and horrible,[13] though mainstream reaction to the "hippies" is also relevant.

Or take the poor, a group that by its very failure to "make it" proves its unworthiness to other Americans. Poverty has always been a problem for those who find themselves in that sorry state. To be poor in a society that stresses success, achievement, and opportunity is an unmitigated disaster. Such a situation subjects one's self-esteem to continuous assault by other members of society. Since Americans generally believe that success or failure depends entirely upon a person's willingness to strive and to work, the poor are generally judged by others to entirely deserve their position. They are failures, it is believed, because of some basic defect in their characters. People on welfare, for instance, are generally believed to be lazy, immersed in drugs, or tied to hoards of babies, produced, so it is assumed, to increase the size of the welfare check.[14] Drawing on these sentiments, and making clever distinctions between the "deserving" and "undeserving poor," the Reagan administration emasculated programs for the poor and near-poor with nary a whimper of protest from other Americans, including most Democratic political leaders. The 1980s were truly "the mean season."

f. Anticommunism. The stress on competition, individualism, the free market, privatism, private property, and limited government feeds the American obsession with communism both at home (where very little of it ever existed) and abroad, manifested in periodic hysteria about the Soviet Union, Cuba, and Nicaragua. Communist doctrine, by seeming to elevate government over the individual, public property over private property, and community needs over private consumption, stands as a living rejection of most of the basic elements of the American belief system.[15] One result of this obsession has been a series of waves of repression of political dissenters on the home front—most notably during the Red Scare after World War I and the McCarthy period after World War II—and periods of induced hostility toward foreign communist states. The latter was particularly marked during the Reagan presidency, generated by his campaigns against the "evil empire" and for the largest military buildup in peacetime history, and sustained by a cooperative media that offered the American people such film and television fare as *Red Dawn*, *Amerika*, *Invasion USA*, and *Rambo II* and *III*.

LIBERAL CULTURE AND THE AMERICAN EXPERIENCE

Although classical liberal thought originated in western Europe and England, it took root most deeply in the United States. In fact, it is only in the United States that liberalism forms the bedrock of the entire culture. In no other society is such homage paid to individualism, to the sacrosanctity of private property, and to the imperative of striving toward success. Nowhere else is "private enterprise" so venerated a term. Nowhere else (with the possible exceptions of South Africa and Chile) does the word "socialism" elicit such fear and loathing—not even in England, the society in which liberal thought was for the most part created (Smith, Ricardo, Hobbes, and Locke were all English) and where the first full-blown capitalist society developed.

Why is this so? What special affinity does the United States have with liberalism? Why is it, in the words of historian Louis Hartz, that "the American way of life" is "the national articulation of the thoughts of John Locke?"[16] Though any answer or set of answers to these questions is bound to be incomplete, some possible reasons follow.

The Protestant Base of the Early American Settlements. A close affinity exists between liberalism and the Protestant Reformation, particularly in their mutual focus on individualism. In America, the liberation from certain religious ties, loyalties, and claims carried over into all of economic and social life. The early settlers of the New World were largely, if not exclusively, Protestant, and in many cases extreme libertarian Protestants.

The Existence of a Lockean Wilderness. Locke based his theoretical work on a hypothetical *state of nature* in which people exercised their labor and ingenuity upon a virgin land provided by God. Since this God-given land was a "commons" available to all, all were entitled to whatever they could individually produce, and in so doing no one would disadvantage or harm anyone else. No such virgin wilderness existed in the world familiar to Locke; Europe and England were characterized either by private ownership of land or by feudal patterns of landholding. In America, however, once the native population had been tricked, expelled, or exterminated, the Lockean wilderness was a reality. The early settlers not only carried the liberal seeds of Protestantism, but they had available to them the raw material upon which to practice that individualism.

The Widespread Ownership of Property in the Early Republic. America was populated with individualistic seekers of private gain who had available to them virtually untouched natural wealth and plentiful, productive land. It is no wonder that within a century and a half of its discovery, North America was a land of yeoman farmers, free artisans, small businesspeople, and a great many property owners. To be sure, neither women nor slaves were offered such opportunities. The society that was to become the United States looked remarkably similar to Locke's imagined state of nature.

The Absence of Competing Political, Social, and Economic Traditions. In Europe, both capitalism and liberalism were forced to fight their way through and against other traditions. Capitalism, for instance, ran contrary both to feudal agricultural organization and to the dominant mercantilist form of international trade. Moreover, capitalism encouraged forms of business behavior (lending money at interest, for example) that ran counter to the ethical teachings of the medieval Catholic church as well as of the early Protestant churches. Liberal ideas, in general, were contrary to the prevailing notions of human nature and to the purposes of government. As a result, while capitalism eventually came to hold sway in western Europe, liberal ideas and values were never totally triumphant there, for liberalism never entirely replaced older modes of thought and behavior. One practical result is that European elites, because of their aristocratic tradition of *noblesse oblige* (a sense of obligation felt by the upper class toward the lower classes), have always been more amenable to social welfare programs than have American elites.

In the European setting, then, both capitalism and liberalism were forced to strike many compromises and were thus diluted from the pure form. In the United States, neither capitalism nor liberalism was faced with any counter-traditions or set of institutions that would soften their influence; they quickly monopolized the American world view.

LIBERAL CULTURE AND CAPITALIST SOCIETY

One of the curious things about liberalism is the evolving divergence between its original theory and actual social reality. The contemporary United States hardly conforms to the Lockean world of small property holders, limited government, and open opportunity. On the contrary, it is a society of giant corporations, bureaucratized and centralized government, wage and salary earners without substantial property, and limited social mobility. The correspondence between the dominant set of ideas and social reality seems increasingly tenuous.

The question then arises: If liberalism no longer helps citizens make sense of their world, why does it remain the repository for the dominant ideas in our political culture? While some would probably suggest *cultural lag* as an explanation—that is, the long lead time required for ideas to change—I would suggest another: Liberal ideas are consciously taught and reinforced, through the institutions of socialization, because liberal ideas support and sustain capitalism and those who control and most benefit from it.

In every society, except during times of turmoil and rapid social change, a rough equilibrium exists between the culture and the principal institutional arrangements of society. In capitalist society, individualistic values are dominant, not communal ones. Likewise, in contemporary socialist societies, individualistic values rank lower than collective ones. This fusion of culture and social structure is never left to chance. The dominant class or group in every society attempts to ensure that appropriate values, norms, and behaviors are taught to the population in general. In most societies, this is done through the main institutions of socialization—religion, education, and communications. The United States is no exception, for schools, churches, and the mass media continually bombard the American people with the tenets of liberal culture. Seen in this light, liberalism is neither "natural" nor "inevitable." It is carefully nurtured.

It is not enough to realize that liberal values remain dominant in American political culture because the principal institutions of socialization continue to teach them. We want to know *why* these institutions do so. If we remind ourselves that institutions of socialization are normally tied to the purposes of the dominant groups or class in any society, this would lead us, in the case of the United States, to look to the capitalist class, and to ask how the diffusion of liberal values throughout society serves its interests. I would suggest that liberalism constitutes a major prop of the modern capitalist order.

Liberalism Legitimates Decision Making by Private Business

Liberalism helps to maintain the legitimacy of private business decision making. Contemporary capitalism is a system in which a handful of people occupying positions of industrial and financial power in the nation's corporations make decisions producing effects far beyond the walls of their particular enterprises. To the extent that liberalism encourages a respect for private property and a general hostility to government intervention in the affairs of private enterprise, it leaves the leaders of these dominant economic institutions free to act on the basis of their own interests. Even though the modern corporation looks nothing at all like the enterprises characteristic of the time of Adam Smith or John Locke, modern business leaders appropriate the language and rhetoric of classical liberalism to protect themselves from unwanted public intrusions. The most important function that liberalism serves here is to establish an artificial separation between politics and economics, to buttress the claim that government has no business in economics (except when it can be of use to the corporation). This separation also places questions related to the distribution of wealth and income into the economic realm, where government is not supposed to roam. By so separating the economic and the political, democracy is thus made safe for economic elites. Its potentially radical implications are eliminated.

Liberalism Encourages Mass Consumption

Capitalism cannot survive without selling an ever-expanding volume of goods and services. It must expand or wither: there are no alternatives. A steady-state, no-growth capitalism is an entity that no one has yet seen and for which no credible theory has been advanced. No growth, or a diminishing rate of growth, in the economy is always occasion for public expressions of worry by political leaders and government economists. The same situation in the private firm causes serious consideration of a change in the management team. For the economy as a whole, no growth means unemployment and underutilization of capacity. For the individual firm, no growth means declining profits, declining market share, and diminishing stock value.

Overall economic growth depends on an ever-expanding consumption of goods and services, either by the government or by the public. The main problem with consumption by the public (unless population is rapidly expanding) is that people are always in danger of becoming satiated, of becoming satisfied with what they have. Worrying about what would happen if the consumer became satisfied, one prominent investment banker made the following observation:

> Clothing would be purchased for its utility value; food would be bought on the basis of economy and nutritional value; automobiles would be stripped to essentials and held by the same owners for the full ten to fifteen years of their useful lives; homes would be built and maintained for their characteristics of shelter, without regard to style, or neighborhood. And what would happen to a market dependent upon new models, new styles, new ideas? [17]

It is with respect to this recurrent problem of capitalist production that classical liberal ideas play their supportive role. Liberalism, let us recall, emphasizes the values of individualism, competition, and striving toward success. At one time, these values helped a vigorous people tame a vast continent. In the

Self-fulfillment: the accumulation of material possessions

modern era, however, in a world of giant bureaucratic organization, economic power concentrated in corporations, and the disappearance of cheap and plentiful land, liberal values can find few such outlets for their expression. The United States is no longer a place in which every person can aspire to be rich or to be president (if that were ever the case). But one place remaining for Americans to express their individuality, their desire to better themselves and to prevail over their fellows, is in the realm of consumption. The individualistic energy of liberal society which once expressed itself in entrepreneurship is now redirected into the prodigious consumption of goods and services. This inclination is nurtured and directed by the advertising that assaults Americans at every turn. Advertising directs these individualistic energies by focusing its messages not on the intrinsic worth of products, but on how their possession can make one the envy of one's neighbors.

Liberal values and capitalist requirements thus join forces in militating against satisfaction with what exists. Liberalism, given its emphasis on competitive individualism, constantly undermines any and all resting points at which people might say "enough is enough," and sends them hurtling into their next binge of consumption. It is precisely because capitalism requires such spending binges that liberalism is of incalculable value in maintaining the present system of production.

Liberalism Undermines Political Movements of the Left

The political Left has always been defined in terms of its support of the idea that government must play a significant role in the management of the economy, with the goal of forcing economic institutions to serve the public interest and to guarantee a more equitable distribution of wealth and income in society. A culture like that of the United States, which is largely defined by classical liberal ideas, represents an extremely unfriendly environment for movements of the Left. This is true for a number of reasons. Liberalism undermines, in advance, collective definitions of problems and their collective solution by the American people. Although it may be reasonably argued that people are poor because they happen to have the wrong skill, or live in the wrong area of the nation, or to have been born the wrong sex or race, people by and large become unemployed and often stay unemployed not because of defects in character, but because of the uncertainties of private investment and resultant fluctuations in the business cycle and long-term structural change in the economy. The causes for most of the economic problems that people suffer lie outside themselves. There is not much they personally can do about them. The most powerful function that liberalism performs for capitalism is to prevent people from realizing this. A people imbued with liberal values will not as a rule see their own situation as derived from the operations of the economy as a whole; rather, they will blame themselves. Such an outcome is useful for the overall system, since it shifts analysis of problems from criticism of dominant groups and institutions to criticism of self:

> I could have been a lot better off but through my own foolishness, I'm not. . . .
> When I came out of the service, my wife had saved a few dollars and I had a few
> bucks. I wanted to have a good time. I'm throwing my money away like

water. . . . I don't feel sorry for myself—what happened, happened, you know. Of course you pay for it. [18]

> You just seem to reach a certain point, and if you don't have it . . . you don't make the grade. I've found that to be true. I always seem to be one step away from a good spot. And it's no one's fault—it's my fault. [19]

It also goes almost without saying that a system of ideas favorable to individual initiative, business, and the primacy of the market mechanism and unfavorable to government and a large public sector must serve as a kind of built-in vaccine against expansion of the welfare state, the collective needs of working people often articulated in the demands of organized labor, and initiatives to impose public purposes on private enterprises. In such a culture, proposals from the political Left are unlikely to be heard or seriously considered. On the rare occasion when the vaccine proves ineffective and proposals that are hostile to business begin to gain a following, the vaccine can be reinvigorated by tying it to the anticommunist strain in the American culture. That is how in the late 1940s the twin threats to dominant groups represented by a powerful and militant labor movement and the presidential campaign of Henry Wallace were neutralized by a campaign of "red baiting."

CONCLUDING REMARKS

We have covered a great deal of ground in this chapter, including a consideration of the meaning of classical liberalism, its origins, its social ramifications, and its ties to capitalism. We have done so not to pursue some arcane and irrelevant academic issue, but to go directly to the heart of the values that define the American political culture and to demonstrate how such values help shape the behavior of the American people and their institutions. Most important, the discussion has demonstrated how classical liberalism arose out of and serves as a major prop and support of the market capitalist economy.

Given the pre-eminence of classical liberal ideas and values, moreover, it is inescapably the case that certain understandings of social justice and democracy have come to prevail in the United States. Liberalism, that is to say, provides an environment that is compatible with certain forms of justice and democracy and incompatible with others. In a society where individual success, striving, self-reliance, and competition are honored, for instance, it is hardly surprising that neither the socialist conception of justice, with its emphasis on substantive equality, nor the classical conservative conception, with its celebration of fixed social places and reward, have much of a chance. Given a society where values of individualism prevail over values of community, and where private interests take precedence over the public interest, moreover, it is hardly surprising that the direct, participatory form of democracy is not much in evidence. Such a culture strongly favors the indirect, representative form, where the ordinary citizen need not take undue time and attention from private pursuits in order to participate in the political process, as well as the pluralist form, where private interests are advanced in the formation of public policy through the conflict, bargaining, and agreements of interest groups.

NOTES

1. Richard P. Young, "Liberalism: The American Creed," in Edward S. Greenberg and Richard P. Young, eds., *American Politics Reconsidered* (Belmont, Calif.: Wadsworth, 1973), p. 18.
2. Bruce C. Johnson, "The Democratic Mirage," in Herbert Reid, ed., *Up the Mainstream: A Critique of Ideology in American Politics and Everyday Life* (New York: David McKay, 1974), p. 185.
3. Louis Hartz, *The Liberal Tradition in America* (New York: Harcourt, Brace & World, 1955), p. 2.
4. Alexis de Tocqueville, *Democracy in America* (New York: Langley Press, 1845), Vol. 2, p. 107.
5. From Thomas Hobbes, *The Leviathan* (Indianapolis: Bobbs-Merrill, 1958; originally published in 1651), ch. 11.
6. John Locke, *Two Treatises of Government* (New York: Mentor, 1965), p. 396.
7. Jefferson substituted "the pursuit of Happiness" for Locke's "property."
8. From Adam Smith, *An Inquiry into the Nature and Causes of the Wealth of Nations* (New York: Modern Library, 1965; originally published in 1776).
9. For an extremely lucid modern statement of this view, see Milton Friedman, *Capitalism and Freedom* (Chicago: University of Chicago Press, 1962).
10. Garry Wills, *Nixon Agonistes: The Crisis of the Self-Made Man* (New York: New American Library, 1970), p. 283.
11. Philip Slater, *The Pursuit of Loneliness* (Boston: Beacon Press, 1970), p. 8.
12. Herbert McClosky and John Zaller, *The American Ethos* (Cambridge, Mass.: Harvard University Press, 1984), pp. 270–271.
13. See Michael Rogin, "Liberal Society and the Indian Question," *Politics and Society* 3 (May 1971), pp. 269–312.
14. Virtually every stereotype about the poor and about welfare recipients has been shown by social scientists to be untrue. For a summary of the research literature, see Fred Bloch et al. (eds.), *The Mean Season* (New York: Pantheon, 1987).
15. Anticommunism is also fed by the strong religious feelings of the American people. For information on the extent of American religious feeling, see Walter Dean Burnham, "Social Stress and Political Response: Religion and the 1980 Election," in Thomas Ferguson and Joel Rogers (eds.), *The Hidden Election* (New York: Pantheon, 1981); and McClosky and Zaller, *The American Ethos*.
16. Hartz, *The Liberal Tradition in America*, p. 11.
17. Paul Mazur, *The Standards We Raise* (New York: Harper & Row, 1953), p. 32, quoted in Paul Baran and Paul Sweezy, *Monopoly Capital* (New York: Monthly Review Press, 1966), p. 124.
18. Quoted in Robert E. Lane, *Political Ideology: Why the American Common Man Believes What He Does* (New York: Free Press, 1962), p. 69.
19. Ibid., p. 70.

SUGGESTIONS FOR FURTHER READING

Robert N. Bellah, et al. HABITS OF THE HEART: INDIVIDUALISM AND CONTENTMENT IN AMERICAN LIFE. *Berkeley: University of California Press, 1985.* An award-winning, in-depth analysis of individualism as the American world view.
Louis Hartz. THE LIBERAL TRADITION IN AMERICA. *New York: Harcourt, Brace & World, 1955.* A view of American history as an unfolding of the liberal tradition.

John Locke. TWO TREATISES OF GOVERNMENT (many editions). The classic statement of the liberal theory of limited government.

C. B. MacPherson. THE POLITICAL THEORY OF POSSESSIVE INDIVIDUALISM. *Oxford: Clarendon Press, 1962.* The classic description of the linkages between early liberal thought and the rise of market capitalism.

Michael Parenti. INVENTING REALITY: THE POLITICS OF THE MASS MEDIA. *New York: St. Martin's, 1986.* A lively and controversial treatment of the dissemination of liberal ideas and anticommunism by the mass media.

Philip Slater. THE PURSUIT OF LONELINESS. *Boston: Beacon Press, 1970.* A powerful critique of liberal society, its heightened loneliness, and absence of community.

Garry Wills. NIXON AGONISTES. *New York: New American Library, 1970.* A biography of Richard Nixon written with the view of Nixon as the prototypical liberal product.

4

The Law,
the Constitution, and
the Supreme Court

THE MYSTIQUE AND BIAS OF THE LAW

This chapter addresses a subject that is so obscured by mythology, wishful thinking, and patent distortion of the facts that the reader is likely to resist efforts to shed some light on a little-understood aspect of American life: the nature of the Constitution and the basic law of the land. Most Americans seem to share the view that no matter what else might be amiss in our country, no matter how unequal the distribution of benefits and burdens in other areas of social, economic, and political life, we remain a society subject to a body of law and a set of legal procedures that are just, fair, and impartial in the long run. In that perpetual process by which Americans judge themselves either superior to or more fortunate than other nations past or present, the themes which are most often encountered are those that stress the wide availability of civil liberties (the freedoms of speech, assembly, religion, and so on, specified in the First Amendment), the equality of all persons before the law irrespective of rank or material situation, and the availability of judicial remedies to abuses in the administration of justice. These qualities, particularly as they are embodied in the actions of the nation's courts, set the United States apart as a unique and superior system in most people's minds. An uncritical, even reverential regard for the legal order exists among the American people; and this regard serves as one of the strongest props of the American system in an era when respect for other political and governmental institutions has seriously eroded. The mystery and symbolism that surround the law make it appear above faction or interest, the embodiment of the will and ideals of the community. Indeed, the law and those institutions attached to it are granted dignity and respect attached to no other governmental institution:

Courtrooms are built to resemble temples; they tend to be dark, richly paneled, and high ceilinged—violating most precepts of the functional design that pervades so many other public structures. The courtroom is built so that attention is focused on the judge who sits on a pedestal above the other participants. No visitor's gallery rises above him; those who work in' the courtroom are not allowed to sit or stand at his level; everyone else operates below him. He is the only official in the courtroom who wears a special costume—a robe. Everyone must rise when he enters or leaves the courtroom. He is addressed as "Your Honor" even though individual attorneys may despise him as a person. Attorneys are considered officers of the court and subject to his discipline; ordinary citizens who come to court for redress of grievances are labeled "petitioners," or if they stand accused of a crime or civil offense, "defendants." Thus architecture, dress, behavior, and language reinforce respect for the law and for the courts.[1]

The Law and Social Classes

To most Americans, law is the glue distilled from generations of human history that holds civilized society together and frees it from the terrors of both arbitrary tyranny and fearful anarchy. What is all too often forgotten is that the law is a human invention, fashioned out of the perceived needs, interests, and actions of particular groups of individuals. Almost invariably, these groups are the very same ones that dominate society in most of its other aspects. Law, that is to say, is a reflection of the domination of society by certain powerful groups, the simple codification of the characteristic power relationships that prevail in any particular society. The law is an instrument for placing the power of government behind the unequal rules and practices of everyday life. In feudal society, for instance, lord and serf faced each other as highly unequal persons and over time worked out habitual and customary ways of relating to each other economically, socially, politically, and religiously. In time, these relationships came to be codified in laws specifying the relationships, and spelling out the rights, duties, and obligations of each of the parties. Similarly in capitalist society, the law comes to embody, protect, and legitimate the domination of the most powerful economic class.

There should be no mystery about all of this. The law was not handed down from Sinai. Law in the United States is the product of the actions of government institutions (legislatures, executives, courts), all of which are significantly influenced by the actions of the most powerful economic groups in the nation and solicitous of their interests. Nor is this view a particularly radical one, for it has long been recognized by theorists friendly to market society. Adam Smith once pointed out that "till there be property there can be no government, the very end of which is to secure wealth, and to defend the rich from the poor." Or as Jeremy Bentham expressed it many years later, "Property and law are born together and must die together. Before the laws there was no property; take away the laws, all property ceases."

Law is thus one of the ways by which those groups that predominate in society, the economy, and government come to legitimate and solidify their position, and make it seem right and proper to the remainder of the population. One can see this manifested in many places within the Anglo-Saxon legal tradition. In that tradition, private property holds an almost sacred place, with many legal protections surrounding its accumulation and use.[2] Roadblocks are placed in the way of both private and public threats to its autonomy. Closely connected to the privileged position of private property in the Anglo-Saxon legal tradition is the sanctity and inviolateness of contract and of the natural liberty to pursue economic self-interest. The invocation of "the general welfare" or the "public interest" against this array of legal protections for the economically powerful has rarely been successful in the United States, and has been so only under unusual sets of circumstances.

THE CONSTITUTION AND PRIVATE PROPERTY

"In the beginning was the Constitution; and the Constitution was with the Founding Fathers; and the Constitution was the Founding Fathers." This, without much exaggeration . . . describes the relationship between the American attitudes toward history and toward the Constitution.[3]

Probably no single institution of American life is as venerated as the Constitution, the founding document of the American Republic. Indeed, we have been virtual "Constitution-worshipers" throughout our entire history as a nation, seeing in the Constitution the firm design not only for our political life and our universally admired government institutions, but also for the legal structure that guarantees a life of equality and liberty for all Americans. The Supreme Court once affirmed this belief in the following grandiloquent terms:

The Constitution is a law for rulers and people, equally in war and in peace, and covers with the shield of its protection all classes of men at all times and under all circumstances (*Ex Parte Milligan*, 1866).

It has never been fashionable to criticize the Constitution in either professional or lay circles. Tampering with it has been almost unheard of during the entire course of our history.[4] Spokespersons for every conceivable political position invoke its name. To denounce one's opponents as acting contrary to the letter or the spirit of the Constitution, or to interpret their proposals as unconstitutional, has been a tempting tactic for adversaries of every persuasion.

The Constitution must be seen in another light if we are to make sense of it. I would suggest that we look at the Constitution as the foundation for a system of government appropriate to a market capitalist economy and to the protection of the highly unequal class structure which prevails in such an economy. It was not intended at its creation as, nor is it today, the foundation for a genuinely democratic political life; it is, rather, the basis for a system in which those who own the main economic and productive assets of society are secure in their control, use, and enjoyment of such assets. The Constitution helps shape a government and a political system in which those with predominant economic power are free, in Adam Smith's words, to "truck, barter, and exchange."

The claim I am making is surely a strong and controversial one, yet I believe it is a claim that is borne out by the language of the Constitution, the substance of its provisions, and its historical usage as defined by the courts and other government bodies. Much of the remainder of this chapter takes up the details of this story.

The Movement
for a Constitutional Convention

People of wealth and property, mainly merchants, financiers, and planters afraid of the radical democratic tendencies unleashed during the American Revolution, initiated the movement to revise the Articles of Confederation and to substitute a document that emphasized a strong, property-respecting, centralized government. To be sure, the Articles of Confederation were deeply flawed as the basis for the formal organization of a new nation-state. Under their terms, the central government was devoid of the power to levy taxes, to regulate economic relations among the states, or to raise an army. They made no provision for any executive authority to carry out the few mandates passed by Congress, depending instead on the voluntary cooperation of the states. Nevertheless, what was most central to the fear of privileged classes in post-Revolutionary America was the responsiveness of state governments to the rising tide of democracy and the possibility that they might eventually turn against economic privilege and demand greater equalization.

Their worst fears were confirmed by the activities of the government of Rhode Island, which, being favorable to the interests of debtors, began to print cheap paper money for the payment of debts. Creditors were not happy with this turn of events. The ratification of the constitution of Pennsylvania, a document with "leveling tendencies" so strong that it has been characterized by historian Samuel Eliot Morison as "the nearest thing to a dictatorship of the proletariat that we have had in North America,"[5] also provoked great alarm among property holders. The triumph of this extremely democratic constitution represented the annihilation of the political power of the old established families, merchants, and landholders of the Philadelphia area, and the rise to political power of the debt-ridden western agrarians. The future Federalist Benjamin Rush felt that the new constitution was "too much upon the democratic order."[6] The possibility that some of the democratic devices of this constitution might spread to other state constitutions further worried the privileged.

Even more dramatic was the fear that struck the wealthy upon the outbreak of populist-style rebellions, particularly Shays's Rebellion. This revolt was a response by small farmers of western Massachusetts, who acted after years of peaceful protest and petition against the heavy taxes imposed by eastern merchants and financial interests. These were designed to pay off the state debt (the notes for which were held by the wealthy). The rebellion struck fear into the hearts of people of property throughout the colonies:

> It was Shays's Rebellion, that militant outbreak of populism that set all Western Massachusetts in uproar, and spread to the very outskirts of Boston, which crystallized the antidemocratic sentiment, and aroused the commercial group to decisive action. With its armed attack upon lawyers and courts, its intimidation of legislators, its appeal for the repudiation of debts, it provided the object lesson in democratic anarchy which the friends of law and order greatly needed. The revolt was put down, but the fear of democracy remained and called aloud for stronger government.[7]

Shays's Rebellion worried men of great wealth in the new nation. John Jay wrote of his uneasiness to George Washington: "Our affairs seem to lead to some crisis, some revolution—something I cannot foresee or conjecture. I am uneasy and apprehensive; more so than during the war." For his part, George Washington wrote to James Madison of his concerns: "If government cannot check these disorders, what security has a man for life, liberty, or property?" Jay and Washington spoke for considerable numbers of their class, because the spread of the news of Shays's Rebellion had the effect of solidifying men of property in all of the colonies in their fear of democratization. Out of this fear arose a desire for a strong national government, complete with a standing army capable of controlling the excesses of the states and random mobs. It is within this context, within this framework of discontent and fear among the well-to-do, that the movement for revision of the Articles swept forward.

The Constitutional Convention

It is clear that the move toward revision and then replacement of the Articles of Confederation was on behalf of those men of considerable property who opposed the further democratization of American society. Let us look at the Constitutional Convention itself—in particular, the composition and views of its membership—and demonstrate that it represented an attempt by the well-to-do to dam the tides of participation unleashed by the widespread dissemination of democratic ideas. A great deal has been written about the Constitutional Convention, especially in response to Charles Beard's *An Economic Interpretation of the Constitution*,[8] which first and most emphatically proposed the class nature of the proceedings. Despite numerous counterattacks by established historians,[9] the weight of evidence still lies with the essence of Beard's arguments (though not necessarily the particulars). The most telling evidence concerning the class nature of the convention is the composition of the delegates and how the delegates interpreted their own roles and objectives.

The men who gathered in Philadelphia to put a lid on democratic excesses were of a particular sort. While they came from different regions of the new nation, spoke with distinctly different accents, and made their living from different lines of work, they were all men of considerable wealth and standing. Nowhere to be found in this august gathering were ordinary mechanics, farmers, and workers; certainly there were no indentured servants or women. Only wealthy merchants, financiers, and planters were there; what they shared was a belief in the Lockean dictum that "the great and chief end of men's uniting into commonwealths, and putting themselves under government, is the preservation of their property."

The delegates knew, furthermore, why they had gathered in Philadelphia; the issues were transparent for all to see. While much of the time was taken up with the question of the relative powers of state and national governments, the essence of the debate actually lay elsewhere for the participants. The Antifederalists (those opposed to the new Constitution) favored only minor changes in the Articles of Confederation, for they saw the states as increasingly democratized and amenable to debtor and small-farmer interests. They correctly perceived, and the proponents of the Constitution admitted, that the move to enhance national power was designed to protect the interests of the property-owning class. Thus the state-national and Articles-Constitution debates reflected class factors. One of the landed participants put the case clearly: "The more we abridge the states of their sovereignty, . . . the more safety, liberty and prosperity will be enjoyed by each of the states." Such a national government "could then be freed from popular control, for were all power held by the people, disorder and tyranny must ensue."

While contemporary historians continue to debate the ideological and class factors dominant among the designers of the Constitution, to the participants themselves there was no question why they had gathered.[10] They had done so to halt what they considered to be the excesses of democracy, and to reestablish a stable climate for business activity and elite governance. One of the participants, a clergyman named Jeremy Belknap, put the issue for his fellows: "Let it stand as a principle that government originates from the people; but let the people be taught . . . that they are not able to govern themselves." The business of the Constitution became that of working out the machinery embodying Belknap's observation.

There is no doubt that most of the participants at the Convention shared Belknap's sentiments. The eminent historian Richard Hofstadter observes that the main theme of the convention was the profound distrust of the common person, and logically, of democratic rule.[11] Historian Vernon Parrington observes that of all the philosophers discussed during the debates, only a handful were democrats. The majority were either aristocratic republicans (who favored a republic ruled by aristocratic elements) or constitutional monarchists. As Alexander Hamilton is reported to have said: "The people, sir, are a great beast."

Historians are also agreed about the other major themes of the debates, in particular the need for a national government with sufficient strength to regulate commerce, halt currency inflation, check the excesses of rebellion and anarchy, and protect against the "leveling" tendencies so feared by Madison. All of these desires put them in conflict with small-property–owning farmers (who, it ought to be stressed, comprised the majority of the free population), who enjoyed their greatest influence at the state level. As Parrington suggests, the need for a strong national state was the basic underlying assumption, along with antidemocratic sentiments, of the Constitutional Convention. As the historian J. Allen Smith once put it, "It was the almost unanimous sentiment of the Convention that the less the people had to do with the government the better."[12]

From Philosophy
to Constitutional Provisions

The logical consequence of these antidemocratic sentiments and of the desire for a strong national government was a search for methods to check majorities and protect the interests of minority property holders. As John Jay so bluntly put it, "The people who *own* the country *ought to govern it.*" While it is the fashion today to interpret minority protection in the Constitution as a means to aid helpless minorities, to the Founders the minorities to be protected were clearly the *propertied* and the *wealthy*. James Madison, rightly called the father of the Constitution, saw the issues in these terms in *The Federalist:*

> In all civilized countries the people fall into different classes having a real or supposed difference of interests. There will be creditors and debtors, farmers, merchants and manufacturers. There will be particularly the distinction of rich and poor.

Given this division, he suggested that the role of government was to check the majority and to protect against "leveling" tendencies that might lead to an "agrarian law." "Wherever the real power in a government lies, there is the danger of oppression. In our government the real power lies in the majority of the community." As Richard Hofstadter has argued, the goal of the Founders was not to extend liberty to slaves and indentured servants, or to protect the civil liberties of the common person. To the framers of the Constitution, *liberty* was linked to property, not to democracy.[13]

> The Convention was a fraternity of types of absentee ownership. All property should be permitted to have its proportionate voice in government. Individual property interests might have to be sacrificed at times, but only for the community of propertied interests. Freedom for property would result in liberty for men—perhaps not for all men, but at least for all worthy men. . . . To protect property is only to protect men in the exercise of their natural faculties. Among the many liberties, therefore, freedom to hold and dispose property is paramount. Democracy, unchecked rule by the masses, is sure to bring arbitrary redistribution of property, destroying the very essence of democracy.[14]

THE STRUCTURE OF THE CONSTITUTION

Given a state of affairs where common people were despised, democracy was feared, and property felt itself under attack in the various states, the convention formulated a constitutional structure which, while providing some safeguards for dissenters and various minority groups, formed a stable legal and governmental base for the development of American capitalism. Let us review some of the major features of that document.

The Creation of a Strong Central Government. The convention was charged by Congress with the task of amending the Articles of Confederation to solve some of their recurrent problems; but it instead reached the momentous decision to substitute an entirely new document establishing a more powerful national government. Given its legal charge from Congress, the national power articulated in the document is truly impressive, even audacious in the scope of its claims.[15]

PREAMBLE:

We the People of the United States in Order to form a more perfect Union, establish Justice, insure domestic Tranquility, provide for the common defence, promote the general Welfare, and secure the Blessings of Liberty to ourselves

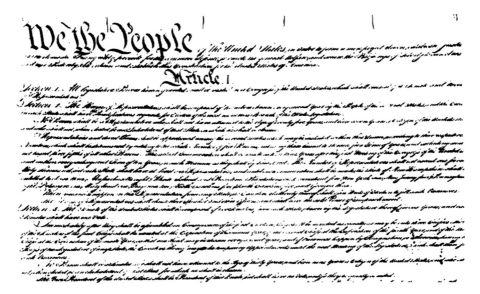

The Constitution of the United States

and our Posterity, do ordain and establish this Constitution for the United States of America.

FROM ARTICLE VI:

This Constitution, and the Laws of the United States which shall be made in Pursuance thereof; and all Treaties made, or which shall be made, under the Authority of the United States, shall be the supreme Law of the Land; and the Judges in every State shall be bound thereby, any Thing in the Constitution or Laws of any State to the Contrary notwithstanding.

Safeguards for Private Property and a Market Economy. Above all else, the purpose of the convention was to provide a framework for the acquisition, use, and transfer of private property, free from the fears of both populist-style intrusions and an unreliable financial and economic environment. A number of provisions speak directly to these needs, some of which provide for domestic order, some of which provide for a stable currency and business environment.

ARTICLE I, SECTION 8:

The Congress shall have power . . . to regulate Commerce with foreign nations, and among the several states and with the Indian tribes; To establish . . . uniform laws on the subject of bankruptcies throughout the United States;
To raise and support armies . . .
To coin money . . .
To provide for organizing, arming, and disciplining the militia. . . .

ARTICLE IV, SECTION 1:

Full faith and credit shall be given in each state to the public Acts, Records, and Judicial Proceedings of every other State. . . .

The latter provision represents not only a powerful statement of the unification of the states into a single nation, but also a defense of the notion of the inviolability of contract, one of the basic building blocks of a national market economy. The Constitution also provides numerous defenses of property against tampering by any level of government. Note, in particular (though it is hidden in rather elaborate language), the protection of property in slaves:

ARTICLE IV, SECTION 2:
No person held to Service or Labour in one State, under the Laws thereof, escaping into another, shall, in Consequence of any Law or Regulation therein, be discharged from such Service or Labour, but shall be delivered up on Claim of the Party to whom such Service or Labour may be due. [16]

Safeguards Against Majority Rule. It has often been pointed out that the genius of the American Constitution rests in its elaborate provisions for the separation of powers and for checks and balances among government institutions. Any judgment as to its genius depends, of course, on an evaluation of the uses to which government has been put. Nevertheless, recall that the overriding concern at the convention was to ensure that the passions of the population would not be permitted to overwhelm the government and move it in possibly dangerous directions. Believing that tyranny results when a majority imposes its will on a minority (property holders), the Founders formulated a series of provisions to ensure that no such majority could easily capture the policy-making machinery of the various branches of government. Such provisions pervade the Constitution and are too numerous to be listed here. Most important, perhaps, the national government is split into three separate branches—the judicial, the executive, and the legislative—each with a distinctly different method for filling its offices, and each with some check on the activity of the others. [17] The president may veto congressional legislation, for instance; while Congress must appropriate funds for presidential activities, approve many executive appointments, and formally approve treaties (in the Senate). Congress depends on the president to carry out its legislative mandates. The judicial branch may judge the legality of executive and legislative activities, yet is itself dependent upon the particulars of its formal organization, upon funding from Congress, and upon the president to enforce its decisions. With such an elaborate intermixing yet separation of the branches, no single branch, it was believed, could act tyrannically. Separated as they were, no popular majority could capture them simultaneously. And since the branches were interdependent, no branch could unilaterally impose its will on the nation.

The Constitution is filled with additional provisions designed to check the unbridled intrusions of a government moved by passionate majority sentiment. The most popular branch, Congress, is itself divided into two houses in order to check hasty and ill-considered legislation, or, to put another face on the issue, to considerably slow down the legislative process. The Senate elects but one-third of its membership at each congressional election, further protecting Congress from tides of popular sentiment. [18] Note also the very difficult process by which the Constitution itself is amended; [19] strong democrats such as Thomas Paine, Thomas Jefferson, and Samuel Adams believed that the fundamental law ought to be easily amended at any time by a majority of citizens. The document, moreover, arranged for the election of the president not through a direct popular vote but through intermediaries (electors), whom the Founders hoped would be the "social betters" in the community.[20]

One Antifederalist characterized the final product of the Convention in the following terms:

> We have thought meet to indulge them in something like a democracy in the new constitution, which part we have designated by the popular name of the House of Representatives; but to guard against every possible danger from this *lower house,* we have subjected every bill they bring forward, to the double negative of our upper house and president—nore have we allowed the populace the right to elect their representatives annually, as usual, lest this body should be too much under the influence and controul of their constituents.[21]

Other Constitutional Features. The Philadelphia conferees formulated a constitutional document whose aim was to create a framework for a strong national government; for a stable, nonthreatening environment protective of property in which a market economy might operate; and finally, for a national government insulated against popular majorities. To a great extent, the Founders succeeded in their efforts, although several of their designs did not work out as intended. Despite the electoral system, for instance, the presidency has emerged as a genuinely popular institution. Through the amendment process, the provision for the indirect election of senators was altered, as was the protection of property in slaves. What is most impressive about the Constitution, in fact, as many scholars and commentators have pointed out, is its historic flexibility, its ability to serve as the foundation of American governmental and political life during radically different times. In the main, its very simplicity and brevity have made it amenable to reinterpretation as the times have demanded it.

The creation of a strong national government, protective of property and insulated against popular majorities, is the heart of the constitutional framework, but does not exhaust all of its features. Two others are particularly worthy of attention: federalism and the Bill of Rights. The Constitution represented a compromise solution at the Convention between those who advocated a centralized government (some even proposed a constitutional monarchy), and those who feared any diminution of power in the state governments. The Constitution effected this compromise by reserving some powers exclusively to the states (such as the specification of electoral qualifications,[22] the conduct of elections, the ratification of the Constitution and its amendment); by reserving certain powers exclusively to the national government (such as the provision of a currency, the regulation of commerce, and the conduct of foreign relations); and by lodging all residual powers in the states (Amendment X: "The powers not delegated to the United States by the Constitution, nor prohibited by it to the States, are reserved to the States respectively, or to the people"). While the relative weight of power has shifted to the national government during our history, particularly during the twentieth century, the United States remains a system in which the powers and responsibilities of government are divided and shared between government levels.

It is also important to mention the Bill of Rights, that section of the Constitution considered its very heart by most Americans, the foundation stone of American liberties. Strangely enough, the Bill of Rights was not a part of the original document as written in Philadelphia at the Convention and transmitted to the states for ratification. Indeed, it was not until the ratification of the Constitution came to be in doubt that its supporters promised to introduce at the First Congress a set of amendments specifying the rights and liberties of Americans, a promise that was kept with the passage of Amendments I through X (ratified December 15, 1791). Much more will be said about the practice and protection of these rights and liberties in a later section.

Ratifying the Constitution

An important question remains: "If the Founders were engaged in an anti-democratic counterrevolution, how did it happen that the Constitution was approved by eleven states within the following year?"[23] In the most extensive analysis yet made of the fight over the ratification, it has been convincingly demonstrated that *sentiment in the majority of states was against ratification of the Constitution.*[24] The answer is really quite simple: The ratification process was itself highly undemocratic, largely controlled by the same people and groups responsible for writing the document. Eminent historian Jackson Turner Main shows that seven states were certainly *against* ratification, three were strongly for it, and three were uncertain. The obvious question is how the Constitution came to be ratified. Main shows that ratification was primarily the product of the superior economic position of the Federalists. The control of wealth allowed them to control most newspapers and thus to play down Antifederalist arguments, feature pro-Constitution writers, and distort the news. False reports were constantly given on, for instance, Federalist strength, the inevitability of Federalist victory, and the support for the Constitution by prominent people (such as Patrick Henry, who was, in fact, a passionate opponent). Wealth also enabled the Federalists to create superior organization, to locate and mobilize their supporters, and to discourage opponents. In almost every state, the Antifederalists gathered too little, too late. Superior wealth also allowed proponents of the Constitution in many cases to resort to economic pressure and intimidation against their opponents. Jackson Turner Main documents innumerable cases of advertiser pressure against Antifederalist newspapers, the bribing of prominent opponents in the states, and the calling-in of notes of Antifederalist debtors. In an interesting preview of contemporary politics, furthermore, voter turnout in the states was extremely low, enabling economically powerful and well-organized groups to wield influence far beyond their numbers. It is useful to remember, finally, that the new Constitution was never ratified by popular vote. Instead, ratification was by state conventions in which the election of delegates was by very limited franchise based on property qualifications. The common people of the time were largely excluded from a ratification process controlled, in the end, by their economic and social superiors.

It is important to note that these observations are not merely the charges of disappointed losers in the struggle, but were affirmed by many Federalists who found the proceedings a bit distasteful, though necessary. A prominent Massachusetts supporter of the Constitution, George Richards Minot, observed that the Federalists were obliged "to pack a Convention whose sense would be different from that of the people." Indeed, Minot titled a long list of Federalist trickery and unethical tactics "bad measures in a good cause."

THE CLASS INTERPRETATION
OF THE CONSTITUTION

Those who, like Charles Beard and Vernon Parrington, argue for a so-called "economic interpretation" of the Constitution (what I would call a "class interpretation") must answer those critics who suggest that while the Founders were surely a very narrow and exceedingly privileged sector of the American population, they were, nevertheless, men of vision, guided by more than their own class interests. Their intent, it has been claimed by their defenders, was to create a governmental system for the ages, broadly democratic yet prudent, and in the end, sensitive to the needs of all classes and social groups. Other than "Fourth of July" rhetoric and unsupported claims of this sort, however, the evidence that is usually marshalled in defense of this position are various demonstrations that the individual members of the Convention did not enjoy immediate economic gains from the specific proposals upon which they voted. These demonstrations are, in the end, but attacks on a "strawman." What is at issue here is not a direct one-to-one relationship between immediate economic interests and elite behavior but an entire structure of relations in which certain dominant groups benefit. As historian Staughton Lynd has so nicely put the issue, "What was at stake for [the Founders] was more than speculative windfalls in securities; it was the question, what kind of society would emerge from the revolution when the dust had settled, and on which class the political center of gravity would come to rest." [25] To the members of the Convention, their purpose was clear. While they disagreed among themselves, often passionately, about how they might achieve their objective, they were nearly unanimous in their desire to protect against "leveling" tendencies and to ensure that "the people who own the country . . . govern it."

It may also be objected that the Constitution, while written with such intentions in mind, nevertheless has become more democratic over the years. To a great extent, this objection is valid; the governmental and political systems have become far more democratic than the Founders could have wanted or imagined. We now elect senators by direct popular vote; the franchise has been expanded by the elimination of property qualifications and the loosening of residency requirements; women and black Americans have been added to the electorate; while the presidency has largely transcended the limitations of the electoral college and become a genuinely popular institution. Nevertheless, it remains the case that our governmental system remains greatly resistant to popular majorities and prone to excruciating periods of stasis and deadlock. The Founders quite consciously created a system of government in which the formulation of coherent national policy would be difficult to achieve, for they feared that such policy, if controlled by popular majorities, would be directed at them and their holdings.

We remain saddled by their creation to the present day. That creation, as political scientist Ted Lowi puts it, is "uniquely designed for maintenance." In the main, the only forces that are generally capable of moving the system out of deadlock are severe crises (as in the Civil War, the Great Depression, and so on) and massive, disruptive social movements.

THE SUPREME COURT, THE CONSTITUTION, AND THE RISE OF CAPITALISM

There is no denying that the Constitution has played an important role in the protection of the liberty of the American people. Nevertheless, and equally important, the Constitution has provided a protective environment for the development of capitalism, which, as we shall see, has had serious adverse consequences for the health, safety, and freedom of the American people. The Supreme Court, as the primary interpreter of the Constitution, has further solidified it over the years as an instrument for the use and protection of the most powerful economic forces in the nation. Some of the most important and lasting contributions to this tradition were made by the Marshall Court in the first three decades of the nineteenth century, which, through a series of landmark decisions, advanced the intentions of the writers of the Constitution and served to shape all later constitutional history.

The Marshall Court. Chief Justice John Marshall was a follower of the doctrines of Alexander Hamilton, who, in his famous "Report on Manufactures" to the Congress, had proposed that the future greatness of the United States must be built on an alliance of a powerful central government and big business. Marshall's aim was to free business from the restraints of state and local governments, to enhance the federal role in interstate commerce, and to thereby help construct an open, vital, national economy. In *McCulloch* v. *Maryland* (1819) the Court affirmed the supremacy of the federal government over state governments by forbidding the state of Maryland to tax a federally chartered United States bank, claiming that "the power to tax is the power to destroy." Of even more interest in that case, the Court decided that Congress had acted properly in creating an institution not mentioned in the body of the Constitution, citing Congress's power "to make all laws necessary and proper for carrying into execution" its other duties and powers (Article I, Section 8). In *Gibbons* v. *Ogden* (1824), the Court further enhanced the powers of the federal government by affirming and clarifying its domination in the regulation of commerce between the states. In *Trustees of Dartmouth College* v. *Woodward* (1819), the Marshall Court held that a corporation was equivalent to a person in the eyes of the law, and was a holder of rights against society and thus protected by the Constitution. For any government to impose social obligations upon the operations of a corporation, to regulate it in the public interest, necessarily intrudes upon its rights as a person who had entered into a valid contract. While Dartmouth College was not a business enterprise, this decision opened the gates to untrammeled and unrestricted free enterprise under corporate auspices later in the nineteenth century. Perhaps the most famous case of the Marshall Court was *Marbury* v. *Madison* (1803), in which the principle was first articulated that the Supreme Court may declare a law passed by Congress or by the states unconstitutional and thus void. In the process, the Court established in law the federalist principle of judicial review, a principle seen at the time as a bastion against the passions of popularly elected legislators. Through this series of landmark cases, the Marshall Court built the legal structure for the supremacy of the national government, the protection of property rights, and the free operations of a capitalist economy.

The Supreme Court and Emerging Capitalism. In the second half of the nineteenth century, the Supreme Court became the virtual handmaiden of the newly emerging industrial corporations. It rendered a series of decisions that reaffirmed their status as persons and holders of rights to be left free from interference in their operations. Moreover, the Court interpreted the *due process* clause ("No state shall make or enforce any law which shall abridge the privileges or immunities of citizens of the United States; nor shall any state deprive any person of life, liberty, or property, without due process of law") of the Fourteenth Amendment, which was originally placed in the Constitution to protect newly enfranchised black citizens in the wake of the Civil War, as a prohibition against state regulation of business corporations and efforts by working people to form labor unions.

The Court also interpreted the Sherman Anti-Trust Act, originally directed toward the problem of monopoly, as a law prohibiting the unionization of workers, for unionization would interfere with the freedom of contract between two

The Supreme Court of the United States

persons—the business corporation and the worker. Finally, in *Pollock* v. *Farmer's Loan and Trust Co.* (1895), the Court invalidated a law in which Congress imposed a tax upon individual incomes. The identification of the Court with national economic interests was so close, in fact, that one New York bank president was moved to toast the Court to an audience of businessmen in 1895 in the following euphoric terms: "I give you, gentlemen, the Supreme Court of the United States—guardian of the dollar, defender of private property, enemy of spoliation, sheer anchor of the Republic!" [26]

The Court and the Depression Watershed. For most of its history, from the era of John Marshall through the 1920s, the Court substantially agreed with the interests and needs of the leading national economic institutions. In the last decades of this era, the Court was particularly active in protecting the corporation from the dual threats of regulation by state governments and a unionized work force. This happy relationship was torn asunder by the events that surrounded the collapse of American capitalism in 1929. The crisis of capitalism was reflected in a crisis for the Supreme Court itself. In response to the Great Depression, the leaders of the most advanced sectors of the business community as well as national political leaders moved in directions sharply at odds with prevailing notions on the Court. While members of the Court remained tied to fairly strict *laissez-faire* notions, corporate and political leaders were becoming sensitive to the necessity of constructing a form of cooperative, corporate capitalism in which the national government would be actively involved in the protection, coordination, and stabilization of the entire economy. When the Roosevelt administration moved in a vigorous way to translate its interpretation into legislation, the Court responded by rejecting many of the landmark programs of the New Deal, the most important ones being minimum wage legislation, the National Industrial Recovery Act, and the Agricultural Adjustment Act. Despite the loud public debate about the "nine old men" of the Supreme Court, the constitutional crisis was short-lived. The Court has never for long been out of step with other national elites. It is impossible to determine the exact causes, but it is striking that with little change in personnel, the Court began to find New Deal legislation perfectly constitutional after 1937, including its new conceptions of governmental activism. Whether this transformation was influenced most centrally by the power of public opinion as reflected in FDR's smashing 1936 electoral victory, by the fear elicited among justices by Roosevelt's ill-fated plan to expand and "pack" the Court with friendly jurists (he was fond of saying that he "lost the battle but won the war"), or by pressures from corporate and financial leaders is largely immaterial. It remains an inescapable fact that after 1937, the Court returned to the elite fold. From that date through the present day, the Court has given the national government a virtual free hand in regulating and coordinating corporate capitalism.

The Court and Dissent. The Court has made another important contribution in linking the Constitution to the interests of private property. Despite a seemingly clear and unambiguous prohibition in the Constitution against any limitation on the exercise of free speech ("Congress shall make no law . . . abridging the freedom of speech"), the Court has been willing throughout its history to allow government a very wide latitude in suppressing the political activities of dissident groups and individuals as well as the free expression of antiproperty ideas. Indeed, from the passage of the Alien and Sedition Acts during the administration of John Adams, up to the present, *the Supreme Court has never declared unconstitutional any act of Congress designed to limit the speech of dissidents.*[27] Nor has it been particularly tough on governmental authorities in their use of police, investigative, and administrative powers against those bold enough to express antisystem points of view. I shall have much more to say about this aspect of the behavior of the Court in the next section.

The Court and Structural Inequality. Over the course of the past three decades, now that the constitutional framework for modern corporate capitalism is firmly in place, the Supreme Court has expanded the rights of criminal defendants and increased the constitutional protections for racial and cultural minorities and women. Nevertheless, these important and significant advances have been confined to expanding procedural rights, guaranteeing equality before the law, and opening the opportunities for the practice of formal citizenship but have not been directed toward establishing substantive and material equality. As such, these advances in no way represent a challenge to the overall structural inequalities in the system between those who own vast amounts of property and those who do not. Thus, while the Court has acted to protect the enjoyment of liberties and opportunities for individuals treated badly by some government entity, it has not, and indeed cannot, act to declare structural conditions of inequality outside of the law; it has not and cannot, that is to say, declare poverty, unequal holdings of private property, and unemployment unconstitutional. While dramatic advances have been made in a great many areas of American life through the actions of the Court, the institutions of corporate capitalism and the system of class inequality remain untouched and intact, with the basic framework of the law acting as one of its most fundamental props.

CIVIL LIBERTY AND DISSENT

The discussion of the Constitution and the role of the Supreme Court in the regulation of dissent and the expression of unpopular views leads us to consider the larger question of civil liberties and their exercise in the United States. To most Americans, what distinguishes the United States from all other societies is that it is a "free society," one in which every individual has the right and the opportunity to hold whatever beliefs he or she chooses, to criticize the government, to publish and to read all manner of opinion on public issues, to associate with others of like mind for the purpose of petitioning the government (or to turn it out in an election), to practice the religion of one's choice, and so on. These liberties are guaranteed to American citizens in the First Amendment to the Constitution, which reads:

> Congress shall make no law respecting an establishment of religion, or prohibit-
> ing the free practice thereof; or abridging the freedom of speech, or of the press;
> or the right of the people peaceably to assemble, and to petition the Govern-
> ment for a redress of grievances.

Our "free society" is constantly and favorably compared (rightly so) to repressive and totalitarian societies like the Soviet Union. Every time a political dissident is jailed or expelled from that country—the cases of author Alexander Solzhenitsyn and physicist Andre Sakharov being the most prominent—editorialists around the country, from big city to rural village, write in almost rhapsodic terms about American freedom. The average American, continually exercising the right to complain, to vote, to move, to worship, and so on, sees the theory of the free society reflected in the reality of his or her life, thus strongly reaffirming the belief in America's special place in the world and in history.

I will not claim in this discussion that the above assertions are simple myths. Civil liberties have been practiced and defended, often quite vigorously, at many times and places in American history. Nor will I belittle the importance of civil liberties, for any decent society must be concerned with the rights and liberties of the individual. Rather, we shall see that the history of the exercise and the protection of civil liberties in the United States is not what it has been cracked up to be. The history of civil liberties in the United States is, in fact, a rather spotty one, fluctuating with changes in the political, social, and economic climate.

This is a most important point, for many political commentators acknowl-edge the many examples of government interference with and suspension of civil liberties to be discussed here. Many will even acknowledge the existence of periods of repression in American history. Nevertheless, most historians and political scientists tend to see such periods as random events, recurrent, yet aberrant and atypical. The "Red Raids" of 1919, for instance, are seen as the product of an attorney general who was an antiradical zealot. McCarthyism is seen as a lamentable but unpredictable accident, the product of a particularly oppor-tunistic senator from Wisconsin. I shall take a diametrically opposed position, one that argues that the history of civil liberties in the United States is *patterned:* that government *allows* their exercise when no threat to dominant power relations is involved, but severely *limits* their exercise when groups or persons seriously threaten the capitalist status quo. Repression—public and private efforts to limit or deny the free exercise of constitutional liberties—while brought to bear only intermittently, stands ready at all times for use, during periods of disorder and discontent, against persons or groups offering a fundamental challenge to the capitalist order.

The Long History of Limitations on Liberty[28]

No sooner had the Founders written the Constitution and attached the Bill of Rights than some of them turned to the task of denying freedom of speech to their opponents. Frightened by the radical ideas set loose by the French Revolution, Federalist leaders at the local, state, and national levels used first the courts and then Congress to silence their critics and maintain social stability. Using the common-law concept of seditious libel in which criticism of sovereign government was considered to be a criminal act, Federalist officials hauled their Republican opponents before the bar and managed to fine and imprison a significant number of them, including the editors of four of the five most important Republican (Jeffersonian) newspapers in the country. Not satisfied with the results, the Federalist-dominated Congress passed the Sedition Act in 1798, which made it illegal to:

> . . . write, print, utter, or publish . . . any false, scandalous and malicious writings against the government of the United States, or either House of Congress . . . or the President with intent to defame . . . or to bring them into contempt or disrepute.

While the Sedition Act proved to be extremely unpopular and contributed to the defeat of the Federalist Party in 1800 and its subsequent decline and collapse, the Supreme Court never rejected the statute or the common-law convictions. Indeed, several of the antifree-speech concepts from the common-law tradition— the "bad tendency" doctrine that allowed prosecution for speech or writing that might lead to disorder at some future time; and the "constructive-intent" doctrine that allowed prosecutors to ascribe intent to writers or speakers who might contribute to later illegal activities by others—continued to be used by the courts until well into the twentieth century.

For much of our history, this attitude and such precedents guided the activities of local, state, and national officials. Dissenters and minorities have been fair game. In many states during our first century, Masons and Jews were barred from public office, juries, and certain professions. Irish Catholics were discriminated against by almost every state, as were members of the Church of Latter Day Saints (Mormons). Laws in various states prohibited any utterances against the institution of slavery or favorable to women's suffrage. Peaceful assemblies by working people to form labor unions in the late nineteenth century were regularly broken up by local and state authorities with the full concurrence of the courts. The same was true for those brave enough to advocate anarchist or socialist ideas in the land of private property and free enterprise. The point of this brief review is to argue that civil liberties in the United States, right from the very moment of its founding as a republic, have been honored more in theory than in practice and that the courts have not been, until very recent times, consistent advocates and protectors of the rights of free speech and assembly. What we shall learn is that, in fact, the expansion of the practice of liberty in the United States came not from the magnanimity of political and economic elites but from democratic pressures from below.

The Many Forms of Repression

Efforts to prevent dissident individuals and groups from freely exercising their liberties have taken a wide variety of forms in American history, from the crudest sorts of vigilante violence to orderly processes in courts of law. The subject of repression in the United States is especially difficult to discuss because it is located in no single, identifiable place. There is no KGB or its equivalent. Repression in the United States is marked by its complex instruments and the decentralized control of these instruments, scattered as they are among various branches of federal, state, and local governments, as well as among private individuals and groups. Let us examine some of the many forms that repression has taken in American life.

Violent Repression. Threats to the status quo have almost always, at some point, been answered by violence from its self-proclaimed or official protectors. When the labor movement was in its infant stages in the late nineteenth century, efforts to organize were almost invariably met by vigilante violence, customarily organized by local businessmen. Given their radical political stance, the Industrial Workers of the World (IWW) were particularly subject to such privately organized violence, especially where they generated large followings. In Bisbee, Arizona, for instance, vigilante mobs forceably deported striking miners and refused to allow them to return. In Butte, Montana, labor organizer Frank Little was lynched by a businessmen's group in 1918. Working people who try to unionize have also been forced to deal with the private police forces of employers (Henry Ford had a particularly tough, brutal, and justly infamous police force for his auto plants), antiunion detective and security agencies such as the Pinkertons, and occasional hired thugs. In their study of violence in American life, Hugh Graham and Ted Gurr point out:

> Most labor violence in American history was not a deliberate tactic of working class organization but a result of forceful employer resistance to worker organization and demands. Companies repeatedly resorted to coercive and sometimes terroristic activities against union organizers and to violent strike-breaking tactics. The violence of employers often provided both model and impetus to counterviolence by workers, leading in many situations to an escalating spiral of violent conflict to the point of military intervention.[29]

Private violence, while often successful in the short run, tends to be distasteful to most Americans, and its overuse very often leads to a growth in sympathy for the victims. Much more acceptable, because it wears the mantle and the trappings of the law, is violent repression practiced by government. Military force has often been used to resolve domestic conflicts in the United States, particularly those conflicts involving labor and business. Almost without exception, such force has been exercised in the interests of property and of corporate management. From the massacre by state militia of striking miners and their families at Ludlow, Colorado, in 1914, to the violent repression of the American Railroad Union by federal troops in the relatively peaceful Pullman strike of 1894, to the numerous National Guard interventions against the CIO in the 1930s, the biases in the use of military force have been unambiguous. This pattern found later expression in the use of the National Guard against urban black populations and antiwar demonstrators during the turmoil of the 1960s.

Much more important than federal troops in the violent repression of dissident and discontented groups in the United States are the police forces of the various states and local communities. The Texas Rangers, for instance, have traditionally been used as an antiunion, antistrike force in that state. Local and state police forces were used extensively against civil rights organizers in the South during the 1960s. On several occasions they were directly implicated in the murder of civil rights workers, as in Philadelphia, Mississippi. The police were also among the major weapons in the violent suppression of the Black Panther Party during the sixties. Not only were members of that party subjected to continual harassment (arrest for minor infractions such as loitering, curfew violations, profanity, jay-walking, malicious behavior, defacing a monument, and so on), but they often faced violent police assault on their homes and meeting places. Between 1967 and 1969, police departments around the country were involved in twenty-one raids and gunfights with members of the party.[30] The most notorious case involved Chicago Black Panther leader Fred Hampton, who was killed in his bed during a police raid in December 1969, a raid purportedly designed to search for illegal weapons. To this date, there is no evidence showing that any shots were fired at the police by Hampton or any of his people.[31] Finally, at least 200 police "Red Squads" operated in American cities during the early and mid-1970s, tied together by the federally funded Law Enforcement Intelligence Unit, whose function seems to have been the disruption of dissident organizations through surveillance, harassment, intimidation, and even violence. The San Diego Red Squad, for instance, financed the violent antiradical activities of various right-wing groups in that city.

Repression Through Government Harassment. The ways in which government can harass and disrupt the activities of dissident groups and organizations while remaining within the letter of the law are seemingly limited only by the ingenuity and imagination of officials. During the period of antiradical hysteria immediately following World War I, guided and justified by a Supreme Court decision defining deportation proceedings as administrative in nature and not punitive, the government used the Immigration and Naturalization Service as an instrument for the mass purge of the leadership of the Socialist Party and of the IWW. During the early 1950s, the period of so-called "McCarthyism," congressional committees ran roughshod over the liberties of many Americans, denying them their rights to free expression, privacy, and due process. Indeed, in only one case during this period (*Watkins* v. *United States*, 1957) did the Supreme Court find these "witch hunts" constitutionally intolerable.[32]

The FBI and J. Edgar Hoover were also very busy during the McCarthyite hysteria. Besides spying on legal groups, planting false information, and otherwise disrupting the political activities of groups and individuals exercising their First Amendment freedoms, Hoover encouraged the American people to report any suspicious acts of their friends and neighbors to the FBI so that the "communist germs" might be eliminated from the American bloodstream. Reflecting on this FBI program, journalist David Caute has observed that:

> The results, in terms of public attitudes, were highly satisfactory. Asked in 1954 whether people should report to the FBI those neighbors or acquaintances they suspected of being Communists, 72 percent of a national cross section replied in the affirmative.[33]

During the civil rights demonstrations of the 1960s, officials regularly, arbitrarily, and without due process terminated the benefits of welfare recipients exercising their First Amendment rights in peaceful demonstrations. Occupants of public housing who were similarly involved often found themselves without shelter.[34] Antiwar activists, even those who had broken no law, were occasionally denied government-funded student loans during the Vietnam War. Police, as already pointed out in the case of the Panthers, exercise wide discretion out on the street, and have a variety of weapons with which to harass dissidents. Their most effective weapon has been the overenforcement of minor laws as a way to prevent gatherings (freedom of association) or the dissemination of leaflets (freedom of speech), usually citing obstructions to traffic, loitering, creating a public nuisance, and so on to support their action. In the interests of public order, police officials regularly deny parade permits to dissident groups, though "patriotic" and civic groups do not seem to have similar problems. Agencies ranging from the local police to the Central Intelligence Agency regularly and as a matter of policy infiltrate, disrupt, and undertake wide-scale surveillance of dissident organizations, practices that most certainly destabilize legal political organizations and undermine public support for them because of their "chilling effects."

The Reagan administration was especially alert to the possible contagious effects of information and ideas and made a major effort to stop the virus before it got out of control. Without congressional approval and with the full concurrence of the nation's highest courts, it attempted to cut off the flow of information from the government, deny America the opportunity to hear critical points of view from foreign visitors, and ensure that American travelers were inoculated against contact with dangerous ideas. Among Attorney General William French Smith's very first official actions upon coming to office in 1981 was to inform all federal agencies that they should be less cooperative and generous in responding to requests for information under the Freedom of Information Act. In 1983, President Reagan issued an executive order establishing a life-time censorship system for over 100,000 federal employees in touch with sensitive or embarrassing information. Under terms of the "ideological exclusionary" clauses of the McCarran-Walter Act (1952), visas to visit the United States were denied to such luminaries as Colombian novelist and Nobel Laureate Gabriel García Marquez (*One Hundred Years of Solitude*), Mexican novelist Carlos Fuentes, apartheid critic Dennis Brutus, Hortensia Allende, widow of slain Chilean President Salvador Allende, philosophers Leszek Kolakowski, Michael Foucault, and Regis Debray, and Italian playwright Dario Fo.[35] President Reagan also issued an executive order banning travel to Cuba for all Americans except journalists, professionals, and scholars (upheld by the Supreme Court in *Regan* v. *Wald*) and conducted highly publicized investigations of groups permitted to travel to Cuba as well as travel agencies arranging such visits. Travelers to Nicaragua during the Reagan years reported continual FBI harassment on their return. The FBI during the Reagan years also conducted a massive campaign of spying, infiltration, and disinformation against groups opposed to U.S. policy in Central America, including CISPES, the National Council of Churches, the Maryknoll Sisters, and the National Education Association.

The list could be extended; most readers probably have seen evidence in their own communities of such official harassment in the face of dissent. It is all too painfully obvious that the liberties spelled out in the First Amendment have a difficult time away from the rarefied chambers of the Supreme Court, even in those rare instances when the Court has acted to support the right of dissent.

Private Sector Harassment. Violent repression, whether by public officials or by private individuals, is a blunt instrument, very often creating sympathy for the victims and providing those same victims with a concrete and readily identifiable target. Official harassment also tends, in the long run, to smack of injustice. Far more effective are those tools of repression in American life that are decentralized and obscure, tools that are seemingly accidental, random, and impersonal, leaving no group or institution accountable or responsible. One of the most effective instruments relates to the precarious employment possibilities of social critics. During the early struggles of working people to organize into unions, labor leaders were regularly *blacklisted*—named on lists compiled by and for employers so that those employers might better guard against accidentally hiring "troublemakers." During the McCarthy era, many actors, directors, and writers were blacklisted from employment in the film industry. During periods as disparate as the Red Scare of 1919, the McCarthy period of the 1950s, and the antiwar movement of the 1960s, many people who expressed unpopular opinions were discharged from their teaching positions in elementary schools, high schools, colleges, and universities. Bar associations during the 1950s routinely disbarred attorneys daring to defend politically unpopular people and organizations. When the Lockheed Aircraft Corporation discharged eighteen employees in 1949 because it could not be certain of their loyalty, the California Supreme Court justified the action on the grounds that loyalty to the United States took precedence over any free-speech rights guaranteed in the California and United States Constitutions.[36]

Repression Through the Legal System. Given the traditional reverence for the law in American society, the most effective device for quiet repression of dissident individuals and organizations is to define their activities as criminal and to transfer their conflict with the dominant powers from the street and the ballot box into the courtroom. Such a transformation is a powerful tool of official repression, for to define certain activities as criminal rather than political accomplishes several things favorable to the status quo.[37] First, "criminalizing" dissent makes it possible to ignore the issues raised by that dissent, to redefine the problem as one that involves the determination of guilt or innocence. In such a setting, the issues are not likely to receive a hearing. Second, "criminalizing" dissent makes it more difficult for dissenters to gain allies for their cause in the larger community. Once persons or groups are officially stigmatized as "criminal," they tend to lose sympathizers. Finally, unless one is armed with a strong character and a powerful supporting ideology, "criminalization" discourages and demoralizes dissident individuals themselves once they find that they are treated as criminals by the police, the courts, and prison personnel. The criminal process isolates people and treats them as individual wrongdoers, cutting them off from the support of their compatriots. As Isaac Balbus puts it:

Because formal rationality [the law] tends to depoliticize the consciousness of the participants, delegitimate their claims and grievances, and militate against alliances between participants and other nonelites or elite moderates, it is likely effectively to minimize revolutionary potential and maximize long-run legitimacy. . . . As such . . . that form of repression . . . most consistent with the long-run legitimacy of the state is repression by formal rationality.[38]

Examples of repression through formal legal processes abound. As a method for combating the influence of the IWW, many states and communities in the early part of the century passed *criminal syndicalist* laws specifically defining IWW activities as criminal and thus transferring their persecution to the courts. At the federal level, the IWW was brought before the courts and its leaders jailed for "conspiracy" against industrial production and the draft because of their militantly outspoken stance against participation in World War I under terms of the Espionage Act of 1917. Socialist leader Eugene Debs was imprisoned under the same law, as were nearly 2,000 other Americans.[39] During the black uprisings of the mid- to late 1960s, "rioters" were treated as common criminals, as persons rioting mainly for "fun and profit,"[40] and a political protest was thereby transformed into a legal question to be dealt with formally and dispassionately. The Cold War era saw a number of statutes passed by Congress, principally the Smith Act, designed to deny political and civil rights to supporters of the Communist Party by making it a crime to *advocate or teach* the overthrow of the government by force. The Supreme Court upheld the conviction of eleven leaders of the Communist Party in *Dennis* v. *United States* (1951) when the petitioners failed to comply with the stringent technical terms of the Smith Act. The Supreme Court has always been a participant, in fact, in the criminalization of radical dissent. In *Pierce* v. *United States* (1920) it upheld the conviction of a man for publishing a Socialist antiwar pamphlet. In *Gitlow* v. *New York* (1925) it upheld the conviction of Gitlow for distributing Communist literature, arguing that "such utterances, by their very nature, involve danger to the public peace and to the security of the state." While the Court has usually reversed these opinions in later cases, what is most significant is their willingness to cooperate with other officials in the repression of dissent during "troublesome" times.

We might also take note of *political trials*, trials which, while ostensibly concerned with the transgression of some statute, are in fact concerned with the control of political dissent. Political trials became especially prominent during the anti–Vietnam War protests and the rise of black militancy. The list is long and familiar—the "Chicago Seven," the "Panther 21," the trial of Dr. Benjamin Spock, the trial of the Berrigans, the Gainesville trial of the leaders of the Vietnam Veterans Against the War, the various trials of Huey P. Newton and Bobby Seale of the Black Panther Party, and so on. It is largely immaterial that in most of these cases, juries found the defendants innocent of all charges, for the court process, given its length and complexity, dissipated the energies and treasuries of the affected dissident organizations, and transferred the attention of their members and their sympathizers from political organizing to the criminal courts. The speed with which juries have acquitted suggests the flimsiness of the prosecution cases, and raises the possibility that the political trial is designed by officials less for conviction than for harassment and disruption.

Civil Liberties and Capitalism

The picture painted above does not conform to our self-image as a free society, one in which people hold liberties that are inviolate, free from interference either by government or by other persons. How is it that such a state of affairs can exist in a society that professes other ideals, and in a culture dominated by liberalism, with its emphasis on individual freedom?[41]

The answer to the first part of the question causes no insurmountable problem, for it might be argued that no political system, whatever its expressed ideals, will freely allow the organization and political activity of those groups whose stated aim is a change in the regime itself and the underlying system of class relations. The western "democracies" do not differ in this regard from other systems, though repression of dissent is largely hidden behind the rhetoric of freedom and the complexities of the legal code.

As to the second part of the question, you must recall the discussion of liberalism in chapter 3. It is an inaccurate reading of the liberal tradition to see it as principally committed to absolute individual freedom. From the very beginning, the focus of the liberal tradition has been upon the *rights of property*—the freedom of individuals to buy, sell, and accumulate property without interference. To Locke, the protection of property is the very reason people come together in the first place to form society, and protecting property becomes the primary function of government. The right to rebel, which is surely the ultimate expression of individual freedom, is limited solely to cases in which property holders are oppressed, in which some government interferes with the inviolable rights of property. In Locke's view, *there is no right of rebellion against property!* Indeed, facing such a threat, governments are justified in suspending all rights and vigorously suppressing it. In Locke's words, faced with such a threat to property rights, ". . . all former ties are cancelled, and all other rights cease, and every one has a right to defend himself and to resist the Aggressor."

At the very core of the liberal tradition is a basic contradiction: a commitment to freedom and liberty combined with a powerful justification of the forcible suppression of threats to the property system. Once we are aware of this contradiction, it should no longer surprise us that liberties are available to American citizens only as long as and to the extent that their practice represents no fundamental challenge to the overall system of power and privilege.

The Continuing Importance of Civil Liberties. I must conclude this discussion with an important qualification. While spokespersons for property were the intellectual fountainhead for the ideas of individual freedom, and while they intended to confine liberty mainly to the propertied class, the ideas proved too powerful and appealing to remain there for very long. The freedoms of expression, movement, and assembly so necessary to the practitioners of early market capitalism were eventually seized upon by those groups in society for whom the freedoms were never intended, and the freedoms thereby took on a more democratic cast.[42] Another way to state this is to point out that civil liberties have not so much been freely granted to the American people by the benevolent actions of elites as those elites have been forced to do so by the actions of popular mass movements. That is to say, throughout our history the formal guarantees of the First Amendment have been given life by the democratic struggles of ordinary Americans. One is reminded of the action which forced the original concession for a Bill of Rights, the fight for the abolition of slavery, the long struggle for women's rights, the brave "free speech" actions of the Industrial Workers of the World in the early part of the century, the civil libertarian aspects of the labor movement, and the struggle for the constitutional rights of black and other minority Americans in the 1960s. Because of the existence of this democratic pressure from below and the resultant expansion in the enjoyment of civil rights and liberties, freedom exists in a certain state of tension in the United States. This tension is the result of the contradiction between the private property and class commitments of the classical liberal tradition and the general belief among the American people that liberties extend beyond large property holders to all citizens. Such a contradiction heightens the government's problem of controlling dissent, for the government must repel threats or potential threats to the social order without unduly transgressing what the population considers the legitimate exercise of liberties. To do so openly and persistently would very likely undermine the legitimacy of the government itself. Civil liberties thus have the unique and peculiar quality of being at one and the same time a prop of capitalism and a potential tool for expanding the freedom of all citizens. Liberal freedoms are at one and the same time a tool of social control and a tool of liberation. How they are used in practice depends heavily on the degree of popular support for the libertarian interpretation of the tradition and on public hostility to government transgressions of agreed-upon limits. Civil liberties thus become ideals well worth fighting for both because of their intrinsic qualities and because they are potential barriers to the full exercise of repression by government.[43]

CONCLUDING REMARKS

We have found that both the letter and the practice of the law in the United States are strongly biased in favor of the interests of powerful economic institutions and individuals. Behind the Fourth of July mystique, the Law Day pronouncements, and the general veneration of the American legal system stands the inescapable reality of unequal power. While none of this implies that the legal order *never* offers protection and sustenance to the weak, or that it may not be better than most other legal orders in the world today, the foregoing discussion may introduce a dose of realism into an area of national life all too often obscured by myopic and wishful thinking.

The discussion also suggests that the basic law and the Constitution are supportive of certain forms of democratic practice and not others—clearly representative and pluralist forms are favored and not the direct, participatory form—and a form of economic system, a capitalist market economy, in which a particular conception of social justice (the classical liberal one) prevails. While the basic law and the Constitution do not forbid the existence of direct participatory democracy in the United States or legislate against the realization of socialist or classical conservative conceptions of social justice, they do stack the deck in important ways against such possibilities.

NOTES

1. From Herbert Jacob, *Justice in America*, 2nd ed. (Boston: Little, Brown, 1972), p. 14, based on the observations of Thurmond W. Arnold, *The Symbols of Government* (New York: Harcourt, Brace, 1935).
2. While the general commitment to property has not wavered, what has changed is the type of property afforded the greatest protection. See Morton Horwitz, *The Transformation of American Law* (Cambridge, Mass.: Harvard University Press, 1977) for a brilliant exposition of the triumph of large-scale over small-scale property in the law as American capitalism was transformed from laissez-faire to concentrated corporate form. Note, furthermore, that property refers to a social relation, e.g., the ability to purchase the labor power of others and to control the process of production (see chapter 5). It does not refer to articles of personal use and consumption.
3. Charles A. Miller, *The Supreme Court and the Uses of History* (Cambridge, Mass.: Harvard University Press, 1969), p. 181.
4. Since the Bill of Rights (Amendments I through X) was adopted by the first Congress over 200 years ago, only 16 amendments have been made in the Constitution.
5. Samuel Eliot Morison, *The Oxford History of the American People* (New York: Oxford University Press, 1965), p. 274.
6. Unless otherwise noted, all direct quotes in this section on the Constitution are from Jackson Turner Main, *The Anti-Federalists* (Chapel Hill: University of North Carolina Press, 1961).
7. Vernon T. Parrington, *Main Currents in American Thought*, Vol. 1 (New York: Harcourt, Brace, 1927), p. 277.
8. Charles Beard, *An Economic Interpretation of the Constitution* (New York: Macmillan, 1913).
9. The leading critiques of the Beardian position are: Robert Brown, *Charles Beard and the Constitution* (Princeton, N.J.: Princeton University Press, 1956); and Forrest McDonald, *We the People: The Economic Origins of the Constitution* (Chicago: University of Chicago Press, 1958).
10. Significantly, many prominent proponents of democracy like Thomas Jefferson and Patrick Henry did not attend the proceedings. The latter is reported to have said in explanation, "I smelt a rat."
11. Richard Hofstadter, *The American Political Tradition* (New York: Knopf, 1948), p. 4.
12. J. Allen Smith, *The Spirit of American Government* (Cambridge, Mass.: Belknap Press, 1907), p. 37.
13. Hofstadter, *The American Political Tradition*, p. 11.
14. Ibid., p. 11.
15. See, for example, Article I, Section 10, which starts with the words "No State shall . . ." and then enumerates a long list of restrictions on the powers of the states.
16. Repealed by the Thirteenth Amendment.
17. Consult the Constitution, a copy of which may be found in the Appendix of this book. For the separation of powers see, in particular, Articles I, II, and III.
18. See Article I for the specification of congressional structure and responsibility.
19. See Article V.
20. See Article II, Section 1.
21. From *Letter of Montezuma*, which appeared in *The Independent Gazetteer*, Philadelphia, October 17, 1787.
22. Benjamin Franklin wanted to eliminate all property qualifications for elections to the

House of Representatives but was unable to gain the support of his fellow delegates for this radical proposal.

23. Robert Dahl, *Pluralist Democracy in the United States* (Chicago: Rand McNally, 1967), p. 32.

24. See Main, *The Anti-Federalists*.

25. Staughton Lynd, *Class Conflict, Slavery, and the United States Constitution* (Indianapolis: Bobbs-Merrill, 1967), quoted in Michael Parenti, *Democracy for the Few* (New York: St. Martin's Press, 1983), p. 70. For a well-argued position opposite to the one taken in this text, see Forrest McDonald, *A Constitutional History of the United States* (New York: Franklin Watt, 1982).

26. Quoted in Ira Katznelson and Mark Kesselman, *The Politics of Power* (New York: Harcourt Brace Jovanovich, 1975), p. 326.

27. Theodore L. Becker, *American Government: Past, Present, Future* (Boston: Allyn & Bacon, 1976), p. 81.

28. On the subject of repression in American history, see Robert Justin Goldstein, *Political Repression in Modern America* (Cambridge, Mass.: Schenkman Publishing Co., Inc.); David Kairys, "Freedom of Speech," in David Kairys (ed.), *The Politics of Law* (New York: Pantheon, 1982); Michael Parenti, *Democracy for the Few* (New York: St. Martin's, 1988), Ch. 8; and Alan Wolfe, *The Seamy Side of Democracy* (New York: David McKay, 1978). Much of the material in this section is based on Wolfe.

29. Hugh D. Graham and Ted R. Gurr, *Violence in America* (New York: Signet, 1971), p. 750.

30. Wolfe, *The Seamy Side of Democracy*, p. 50.

31. The FBI was intimately involved in Hampton's murder. The Black Panther chief of security was, in fact, an FBI informer and the source of all information supplied to the Chicago police. As *The New York Times* reported (May 7, 1976), "Within days of the raid . . . the Chicago FBI office asked Washington headquarters for a $300 bonus for O'Neal [the informer] . . . and [he] subsequently received the money."

32. For the most complete compilation of the horrors of the McCarthy period, see David Caute, *The Great Fear: The Anti-Communist Purge Under Truman and Eisenhower* (New York: Simon & Schuster, 1978). Historian Ellen Schrecker shows in her *No Ivory Tower* (New York: Oxford University Press, 1986) that even American universities succumbed to the Red Scare.

33. Ibid., p. 121.

34. Frances Fox Piven and Richard Cloward, *Regulating the Poor* (New York: Pantheon, 1971).

35. Democratic administrations have also used visa control as a way to keep dangerous ideas from infecting the American people. Note the Carter administration's refusal to issue visas to the eminent scholars Ernst Mandel and P. T. Bottomore.

36. Caute, *The Great Fear*, p. 368.

37. Based on Isaac Balbus, *The Dialectics of Legal Repression* (New York: Russell Sage, 1973), p. 12.

38. Ibid., p. 14.

39. The Espionage Act was held to be constitutional in the famous case of *Schenck* v. *United States*, in which the supposed great civil libertarian justice Oliver Wendell Holmes enunciated his landmark "clear and present danger" concept. In upholding the conviction of Mr. Schenck, who had been distributing leaflets condemning the war and demanding that the draft law be repealed (he did not advocate any illegal or disruptive actions), Holmes indicated that Schenck's customary free speech rights had no constitutional protection during a war when such speech has the "clear and

present danger" of producing "the substantive evils that Congress has a right to prevent." So much for "Congress shall make no law . . . ."

40. The quote is a chapter title from the notorious book by Edward Banfield, *The Unheavenly City* (Boston: Little, Brown, 1968).

41. Wolfe, *The Seamy Side of Democracy*, p. 6. Much of the remaining discussion is based on Wolfe.

42. For this history, see C. B. MacPherson, *The Real World of Democracy* (Oxford: Clarendon Press, 1965), and Kairys, "Freedom of Speech."

43. This chapter has focused on issues related to the fundamental law: the Constitution, the interpretation of the Constitution by the Supreme Court, and the status of civil liberties in the United States. The discussion has continually emphasized that the law is not neutral but is, rather, an instrument of and a creation of the institutions of private economic power. It is important to point out that the more mundane, everyday practice of civil and criminal law is also deeply biased in favor of large-scale property and against the poor and the politically powerless. For an introduction to a vast literature on the subject, see Jerold S. Auerbach, *Unequal Justice* (New York: Oxford University Press, 1976); Herbert Jacob, *Justice in America* (Boston: Little, Brown, 1978); Leonard Downie, Jr., *Justice Denied* (New York: Praeger, 1971); David Kairys, *The Politics of Law* (New York: Pantheon, 1982); Richard Quinney, ed., *Criminal Justice in America* (Boston: Little, Brown, 1974); Jeffrey Reiman, *The Rich Get Richer and the Poor Get Prison* (New York: Wiley, 1979); and Edwin H. Sutherland's classic, *White Collar Crime* (New York: Dryden Press, 1949).

SUGGESTIONS FOR FURTHER READING

David Caute. THE GREAT FEAR: THE ANTI-COMMUNIST PURGE UNDER TRUMAN AND EISENHOWER. *New York: Simon & Schuster, 1978.* The most complete (and chilling) catalogue of government suppression of civil liberties in the United States during the McCarthy period.

Edward S. Corwin. THE CONSTITUTION AND WHAT IT MEANS TODAY, 13th ed. *Princeton, N.J.: Princeton University Press, 1974.* A classic work that reviews the history of Supreme Court interpretation of the Constitution.

Robert Justin Goldstein. POLITICAL REPRESSION IN MODERN AMERICA. *Cambridge: Schenkman, 1978.* The most complete treatment of the subject of repression in the scholarly literature.

Alexander Hamilton, James Madison, and John Jay. THE FEDERALIST PAPERS, ed. by Clinton Rossiter. *New York: McLean, 1788; New American Library, 1961.* A brilliant and detailed defense of each of the provisions of the Constitution executed by three people actively involved in its writing.

Nat Hentoff. THE FIRST FREEDOM: THE TUMULTUOUS HISTORY OF FREE SPEECH IN AMERICA. *New York: Delacorte Press, 1980.* A popular treatment of the struggle to make the guarantees of the First Amendment real in American history.

Morton Horwitz. THE TRANSFORMATION OF AMERICAN LAW. *Cambridge: Harvard University Press, 1977.* A brilliant and justly honored book, which examines how changes in the early American economy led to transformations in the case law and in the legal profession.

Herbert Jacob. JUSTICE IN AMERICA, 4th ed. *Boston: Little, Brown, 1984.* A highly respected review of the court system, which has rightly become a standard work in the field.

David Kairys (ed.). THE POLITICS OF LAW. *New York: Pantheon, 1982.* A collection of essays by radical legal scholars which examines basic legal concepts of the American system, from torts to contracts.

Victor Navasky. NAMING NAMES. *New York: Viking Press, 1980.* A penetrating analysis of the McCarthy era and the creation of a culture of informers.

Eve Pell. THE BIG CHILL. *Boston: Beacon Press, 1984.* The story of efforts by the Reagan administration to suppress information and narrow the practice of First Amendment freedoms.

Ellen Schrecker. NO IVORY TOWER. *New York: Oxford University Press, 1986.* The depressing story of the complicity of American universities in the McCarthy-era hysteria.

5

Capitalism:
Theory and Implications

We have now examined the political, cultural, and constitutional/legal foundations of American society. I have argued that both our culture and our legal system are profoundly shaped by their location within a capitalist market economy. It remains for us to ask about the nature of such an economy.

What is capitalism? What are its fundamental characteristics? How does capitalism differ from other economic systems? Does capitalism affect the possibilities for realizing democracy and social justice? This chapter will examine these complex questions. If the discussion seems unduly abstract and theoretical, rest assured that without an understanding of capitalism as a system, the remainder of the book and, I must add, American political life will remain incomprehensible.[1]

CAPITALISM AND ITS RAMIFICATIONS

As a start, I offer the following definition from economist Howard Sherman. In the remainder of the chapter, I flesh out this definitional skeleton and examine some of its implications.

> Capitalism may be defined as an economic system in which one class of individuals ("capitalists") owns the means of production ("capital" goods, such as factories and machinery), hires another class of individuals who own nothing productive but their power to labor ("workers"), and engages in production and sales in order to make private profits.[2]

Some have suggested that modern capitalism is so different from eighteenth-century small-scale competitive capitalism that it is an entirely new creature, free from the problems of early capitalism and deserving of a new name. Hence, the widespread use of terms such as "postcapitalism" or "neocapitalism," or free enterprise. Certainly capitalism has changed rather dramatically over the past two centuries. Nevertheless, it remains an economic system characterized by a dichotomously organized class structure based on the division between ownership and nonownership of property, and by a system of market-oriented production for profit.

Such a definition is not merely of academic interest. It serves to distinguish capitalism from other forms of economic society (both industrial and non-industrial) and to introduce a consideration of certain social problems associated with all capitalist systems, whether free market capitalism of seventeenth-century England or modern corporate capitalism of late twentieth-century America. I shall argue that the essential, defining characteristics of capitalism—the very way it organizes economic life—inescapably entail severe social and human costs. Market production and the class system, by their very nature, have problems and dislocations that are impossible to evade. One of the most important functions of twentieth-century governments has been to alleviate some of these problems and dislocations.

Capitalism is, then, a social system characterized by a class system based on the ownership of property, and by the production of goods and services for sale in the marketplace. The following discussion elaborates and expands the minimal definition of capitalism already presented, and points out some of its most telling social costs and problems.

THE CLASS SYSTEM

Capitalism is a form of economic society in which a relative handful of people own the means by which goods and services are produced and distributed. In this respect, capitalism is not unique. With the exception of some primitive communal societies described by historians and anthropologists, all known historical societies have been characterized by minority ownership of fundamental resources. In classical Roman and Greek society, for instance, only a wealthy and powerful minority of the people owned slaves, the main productive instruments of economic life. In European feudal society, only a tiny minority owned land, the key economic component for agricultural society. In capitalist society, only a small segment of the population owns the main instruments of economic life: factories, machinery, natural resources, land, and investment capital.

Capitalism is a form of economic society in which the owning class, by virtue of its control over the productive assets of society, determines the overall shape and development of economic life. Whether we refer to the era of small-scale capitalists described by Adam Smith or to the current era of giant multinational corporations, the shape of economic and social life in capitalist societies is, in the main, determined by thousands upon thousands of private investment decisions. These decisions encompass such diverse activities as plant location,[3] job design, technological innovation, savings, advertising, and lending. Economic life, which is by nature social and interdependent, is determined by the sum total of the decisions of the owning class and not by the population as a whole through democratic procedures. As economic assets become more concentrated during the course of capitalist development, this decision-making capacity comes to be lodged in ever-fewer hands. Thus, the decisions that affect the affairs and prospects of society in general are made by economically powerful private individuals who are in no way publicly accountable for their actions.

Capitalism is a form of economic society in which the vast majority of the population, not being owners of the productive assets of society, must sell its labor skills, effort, creativity, and time to the owning class in return for wages and salaries. Capitalism is a system in which a minority of people is able to purchase the labor power of others, and is thereby able to determine the purposes and uses of that labor. It is a system in which a few have the means to buy labor and set it to work. It is a system in which the nonowning majority works for ends and in ways determined by the property-owning minority. Indeed, we may best define *private property* not as a collection of things but as the ability to buy and live off the labor power of others. Historian R. H. Tawney has made the following observation about early twentieth-century Britain, and it holds just as well for the contemporary United States:

> Regarded as an economic engine, the structure of English society is simpler than that of some more primitive communities. . . . The most salient characteristic of its class structures is the division between the majority who work for wages, but who do not own or direct, and the minority who own the material apparatus of industry and determine industrial organization and policy.[4]

Obviously, the nonowning majority of the population does not sell its labor skills, efforts, creativity, and time for the sheer joy of being directed by others, but is forced to do so by the need to make a living. Particularly in the modern corporate era, with the decline of small business opportunities, few have the opportunity to become owners in their own right, and most must work for others. This transformation of the vast majority of the population into wage laborers is one of the most salient features of capitalist development.

Capitalism is a form of economic society in which the production of the many is appropriated by the few. Capitalism is an economic system whose lifeblood is profit. Without profit, or the prospect of profit, private persons would be either unwilling or unable to invest their surplus savings in business enterprises, a situation that would inevitably lead to stagnation or collapse. Firms within a capitalist economy constantly seek a level of profitability that allows them to maintain themselves or to expand. This outcome is made possible only by keeping the costs of production (the costs of plant and equipment, raw materials, labor, and so on) significantly below the selling price of the goods or services produced. It is necessary for capitalist enterprises, from one point of view, to give back to the workers, who directly produce some product or service, *less than the value produced*. For a firm to do otherwise would be suicidal. At the level of society, it is necessary in capitalism that the owning class give back to the working class less in wages and salaries than it realizes from the sale of goods and services. It follows that no matter what the absolute level of wages and salaries may be, either in the firm or in the economy as a whole, the relationship of workers to owners in capitalism is one of continuous and perpetual exploitation, in the sense that some portion of the value produced by workers is continuously extracted by those who own but do not themselves produce.[5] It is a system described by Tawney as one characterized by that strange "alchemy by which a gentleman who has never seen a coal mine distils the contents of that place of gloom into elegant chambers in London and a house in the country."[6]

Classes and Exploitation

Exploitation, defined as the power of capital to direct production and to live off the labor of others, finds expression in a variety of forms. Consider the issue of inequality. The most obvious benefit to be derived from ownership is that the bulk of the fruits of the economy flow to those who own. All capitalist societies, as a result, are characterized by severe inequalities in income distribution based on the division, primarily, between those who own substantial capital and those who do not. (See chapter 6 for a more extensive discussion of this issue.) Since access to those goods and services necessary for a decent life are generally available in the United States only to those who can afford to pay for them out of pocket, inequalities of wealth and income are reproduced in most other areas of life. The inegalitarian realities of property are neatly reproduced in such areas as health, education, safety, security, and life style. In a society where most goods and services are available to the highest bidder, it is only natural that those persons with the greatest disposable income enjoy most of the fruits of the economic system.[7]

Whatever its level of affluence and material wealth, capitalism is an inherently exploitative system. Political philosopher C. B. MacPherson has proposed that a society without exploitation would be one in which all persons would have both the opportunity and the means to use and to develop their innate human capacities. He points out that many factors can stand in the way of such development. But above all other obstacles is the lack of access to the facilities for laboring. The development of human capacities requires, as a first order of priority, materials and tools with which to work. The sculptor requires marble and chisels; the architect, T-square and pen; the builder, boards, nails, and hammer. In capitalist society, however, the tools, materials, and other resources requisite to creative and fulfilling work are owned by the few, who retain the economic and legal power to define the purposes for which they can be used. Thus the uneven distribution of property is reflected in the uneven distribution of the opportunity to use and develop capacities. This transfer of human power, as MacPherson points out, is a continuous and inherent one in the relationship between owners of property and sellers of labor. It is exploitative in the sense that one group of people controls access to the means for the development and fulfillment of others.[8]

The relationship is exploitative in another, closely related way. Ownership of property wealth confers upon a relative handful of people the means and ability to determine vital elements of other people's lives. For instance, in capitalist societies, owning and controlling a factory gives one the legal right to determine the technical organization of production and the content of work. Nonowners in such a setting (the situation of most Americans) must work for objectives that are not necessarily their own, produce things not necessarily of their choice, and use their skills and creative talents in ways determined by others.

For most people, this has meant working at jobs that are increasingly frag-

Modern Times: *human beings as appendages to the productive process*

mented, simplified, routinized, and supervised in the name of efficiency and productivity. This has devastating implications for many American workers.[9] If *Homo sapiens* is by nature a free, creative, and independent being, then to work in settings that are controlled, specialized, and routinized is to spend one's life in a manner less than human.[10] Over the past few years, wide-ranging research literature has confirmed that modern forms of work organization tend to run counter to the psychological well-being of most people.[11]

Studs Terkel, in writing about the work experiences of Americans he had intensively interviewed, gives his overall impressions in these words:

> This book, being about work, is, by its very nature, about violence—to the spirit as to the body. It is about ulcers as well as accidents, about shouting matches as well as fistfights, about nervous breakdowns as well as kicking the dog around. It is, above all, about daily humiliations. To survive the day is triumph enough for the walking wounded among the great many of us.[12]

The devastating effects of working class loss of control over the forms and purposes of work was even noted by Adam Smith:

> The understandings of the greater part of men are necessarily formed by their ordinary employments. The man whose whole life is spent in performing a few simple operations . . . has no occasion to exert his understanding, or to exercise his invention in finding out expedients for removing difficulties which never occur. He naturally loses, therefore, the habit of such exertion, and generally becomes as stupid and ignorant as it is possible for a human creature to become.[13]

It is important to note that the relationship between the owner of capital who buys labor and the worker who sells labor is neither accidentally nor occasionally exploitative, but is so in the very nature of class relationships. The relationship, that is to say, is inherently *antagonistic*. Thus, for owners of capital to significantly increase their profits, it is necessary for them to keep a lid on wage and salary rates—or in the modern parlance, increase productivity (for example, producing more from each worker at a constant labor cost, or producing the same amount while reducing labor costs). For the working class to significantly enhance its position in the total economy, it would have to keep for itself a large part of what normally finds its way into profits. For the working class to escape alienating and dehumanizing work settings, furthermore, it would have to break the monopoly of the capitalist class over the organization of the workplace. In contrast to the usual rhetoric that pervades American thinking (which articulates a vision of unity, commonality, and "one big family"), the interests of owners and the interests of workers are perpetually and fundamentally at odds.

The social class concept—the division of society into two great strata defined by their relationship to the system of production, one *owning* and controlling the means of material production and appropriating the surplus created by others, the other *selling* its labor and producing surplus—is the bedrock of my point of view in the analysis of capitalist society. We shall see throughout the remainder of this book how this class division profoundly shapes American politics and public policy. [14]

PRODUCTION FOR THE MARKET

The pervasiveness and importance of the market mechanism is unique to capitalism. The objective of economic actors in capitalism is to produce goods and services for sale in the market. The objective of economic actors is not to produce goods and services to be used by those who actually make them, or to fulfill some direct human or social need. Rather, the objective is the production of things for sale in the marketplace for the *purpose of generating profits*. The drive of capitalist economic life is not toward the useful or beneficial (though since Adam Smith the common assumption has been that such is the normal byproduct of a market system), but toward the marketable and profitable.

Actually, the existence of an all-pervasive market is a rather rare and recent phenomenon in human history. While exchange of goods and services has probably existed in some form in all societies, capitalism is unique to the extent that the market encompasses everything. Under capitalism, for the first time in human history everything is for sale and has a price, including land and human beings themselves. In traditional cultures, for instance, land is regarded as something holy and sacred, the basis of social life, the link to ancestors, the provider of sustenance, the connector of humans to the natural world. As such, land is not something to be bought and sold in the marketplace. One might just as well sell one's arms, or legs, or children in such societies. Similarly, in traditional cultures individuals do not exist as separate and isolated beings but as members of a tightly knit community, connected to the life of the community through family, work, ritual, and ceremony. In such societies, it would be inconceivable to consider human labor as something to be priced in the market-place, to be bought and sold like so many oranges, to be discarded onto the dungheap of unemployment when no one is willing to buy it.

The Transition to Capitalism

As the reader might suspect, both the contact of modern capitalist societies with traditional ones (for instance, the United States in Vietnam)[15] and the transformation of a traditional society to a capitalist one are disruptive, disorienting, and even devastating to the members of a traditional society. This was evident in the transformation of European feudalism into market capitalism. The brutality of this transformation is seen most clearly in the *enclosure movement* of seventeenth- and eighteenth-century England at the very beginnings of the capitalist economy. Over these two centuries, the scattered fields that poor but relatively free farmers had worked by traditional feudal right were gathered together into great estates under single owners, enclosed by hedges and fences, and turned over to the raising of sheep. In the process, agriculture was transformed from the production of *use values* (farm products to be consumed by the largely self-sufficient local community), to *exchange values* (wool to be bought and sold in the marketplace). In the process, the rural population was ripped from the land and transformed into a landless mass, "free" to sell its labor in urban centers. The alternative was starvation, the poorhouse, or forced labor. The process was so disruptive and brutal that Sir Thomas More was moved to lament that "sheep are eating men."

Similar stories can be told of all transformations to capitalism. What is so disruptive about the introduction of capitalism is its tendency to destroy all preexisting traditional forms, so that all elements of the social order become marketable commodities. In describing the transition of European societies from feudal to market in form, historian Karl Polanyi wrote that while such an organization of economic and social life was more often than not conducive to miraculous new heights of production, it "was accompanied by a catastrophic dislocation of the lives of the common people." By subjecting every element of society to the market, including individuals in their own labor, it "annihilate[d] all organic forms of existence and . . . replace[d] them by a different type of organization, an atomistic and individualistic one."[16]

Contemporary Problems of the Market

Readers might protest that if such descriptions capture the barbarism of the early transformation to capitalism, they no longer make sense of the fully developed, mature capitalism of our own day. To a great extent, the objection is well-founded. This may be so because most remnants of traditional society have all but disappeared from western nations under the steamroller of capitalist development. Nevertheless, the market continues to have fully as many negative effects in our own day, though they may be less obvious. A system of production for profit, while enormously productive, leads to a set of severe social dysfunctions. Let me review just a few.

Business Cycle Instability. Capitalism is inescapably subject to periodic economic crises. While western governments have, to some degree, enhanced their ability to manage the business cycle, capitalism remains a system wracked by periodic alterations between recession and inflation, and forever threatened by collapse into depression. Since business investment remains in private hands, directed toward the generation of profit, such investment fluctuates as business-people assess the future possibilities of profit. If the profit picture is not encouraging, the rational businessperson saves rather than invests. Businesspeople, even when they choose to invest, may put their money into unproductive activities (such as real estate speculation and corporate takeovers, so popular in the eighties) or into other countries. Should this tendency toward noninvestment or investment in nonproductive activities become generalized throughout the entire economy, economic activity slows and factories cut back their operations or close. In an economy in which labor is a commodity, workers are then thrown onto the unemployment rolls. As unemployment rises and as other workers find themselves on reduced hours, the level of consumption in the economy further drops, deepening the recessionary spiral, encouraging more plant shutdowns and layoffs.

As recovery begins, either because of new business investment or, more frequently, because of the economic stimulation of massive government spending as in the Reagan boom of 1983,[17] businesspeople with a large pool of savings from the previous period begin to accelerate their level of investment as the overall profit picture brightens. At this point, two things happen. First, the combination of government spending and new investment soon outstrips the capacity of the system to produce goods, creating serious inflation.[18] At a later stage of the recovery, as production accelerates because of the attractive high prices available for goods, production at some point outdistances the effective demand for goods, leaving excessively large inventories. The next collapse into recession or depression comes as businesspeople throughout the economy cancel orders for new goods, factories slow production or close, workers are laid off, and so on as the cycle repeats itself. The violent up-and-down swings of the business cycle are characteristic of any and all capitalist societies.[19]

Workplace Tensions. Since labor in capitalism is a commodity to be bought when needed and discarded when no longer required, and since this market relationship leads to highly disproportionate power in the workplace, capitalism is continuously beset by serious tensions at the point of production. Forced to work for ends and in ways not freely chosen by them, workers customarily express their alienation in absenteeism, low motivation, turn-over, slow-downs, and strikes. This not only seriously impairs production, but also forces the creation of an elaborate, top-heavy, and very expensive supervisory structure to keep the production process going.[20]

Externalities. In order to maximize profits, the capitalist firm attempts to keep its production costs to a minimum. Such costs normally include the price of plants and equipment, raw materials, and labor. Unless it has some perverse desire to lower its level of profit, no rational firm chooses to pay for the social costs or *external diseconomies* of its operations. In order to maximize profits, the firm must ignore the social costs of its activities (whether these costs be pollution, traffic deaths, broken families, or lung cancer) and allow society at large to foot the bill.[21] Unless forced by public or union action, for instance, individual firms rarely—and never at the expense of profit—choose to pay for the damages caused by industrial pollution. To do so would be clearly irrational according to business logic. Unless forced, individual firms rarely make their operations as safe as they might be, given the state of technology; to alter operations in the interests of safety would diminish profits. Such business logic largely explains why the United States, by many measures the world's richest society, suffers by far the highest rates of occupational disease, injury, and death in the industrialized world.

The logic of profit maximization is antisocial because it compels business firms to disregard externalities. Any firm that disregarded its own profit statement out of some sense of social obligation would risk financial disaster or takeover by another firm. Clearly, the issue here is not the goodness or evil of the owners or managers of the firm, but rather the imperatives of any firm in a capitalist market economy.

Waste. Capitalism tends to utilize resources in a highly wasteful and irrational manner. Capitalism remains a system driven by the pursuit of profit. It matters not what is produced and sold, whether it be video games or mass transportation, designer label clothing or medical care, nonreturnable bottles or decent housing, so long as profits are made. In the eloquent and revealing words of one car executive, "at GM we produce profits, not cars."[22]

The irrationality and waste of such a system is surely self-evident. A rational firm, in attempting to make profits in the marketplace, will use whatever methods, produce whatever commodities, and utilize whatever raw materials are required for making profits. The firm cannot allow issues of social waste and irrationality to enter into its calculations, unless they will somehow affect the long-range profit picture of the firm. As a result, the general trend in American industry, agriculture, and transportation in recent years has been to change from the use of relatively efficient, nonpolluting forms of energy to less efficient, polluting ones. Synthetic detergents have largely replaced soap, trucks have largely replaced railroads in shipping, cars have replaced rail travel in public transport,[23] and synthetic fibers have replaced natural ones.[24] Business firms have made such transitions not necessarily out of technological imperatives, but because of essentially correct calculations that more profits were to be made. The effects have been disastrous. While the American population increased 126 percent between 1946 and 1971, for instance, the pollution levels in that same period rose, by some estimates, 2,000 percent.[25] The point here is that what may be rational for the business firm is often wasteful and irrational from a social point of view.

Planned obsolescence is another example of waste. The health of market economies depends on a continual willingness of people to buy goods and services. Therefore, any widespread satisfaction with what one already possesses would be a serious development indeed. Capitalism has evolved a useful method to undermine any such threat to mass consumption: a planned abbreviated life for products. It is a not very well-kept secret that most consumer durable products (such as cars, refrigerators, and washing machines) could, given present technology, be made long-lasting and easily repairable. Such a development, of course, would considerably limit the market for new consumer durables as well as for spare parts. Thus, companies not only ignore such improvements, but actually build a maximum life into their products. The first fluorescent light bulbs had a life of 10,000 hours, a period of useful life much too long from the point of view of the Philips Trust (the patent holder). After much investment of time and money, its scientists were able to reduce the life of the fluorescent bulb to 1,000 hours. It was only at that point that Philips felt sufficiently secure about its long-range profit picture to market the bulb. [26]

Capitalism also attempts to accelerate product changeover through advertising and periodic model changes. These are designed to create dissatisfaction in the potential consumer, who is made to feel old-fashioned, a failure as a provider, or deficient in sex appeal without the new model. In addition to the obvious cost of advertising and of retooling industry to produce slightly different models of standard products, valuable resources are wasted as Americans are encouraged to discard older models. Again, what might be rational from the point of view of the firm, or from the point of view of the capitalist economy as a whole, is clearly irrational and wasteful from a human or social point of view.

Finally, capitalism is irrational and wasteful because it conceives of human labor as a commodity to be bought and sold in the marketplace like any other commodity. Because labor is used only if some enterprise is willing to buy it, persistent unemployment is a central characteristic of any and all capitalist societies, especially in the modern corporate economy (as will be seen in a later chapter), where overproduction and underconsumption become ever more serious, and where unemployment as a consequence tends to fluctuate between 6 and 10 percent of the workforce in the best of times.

To understand the relationship between a market system and waste, it is crucial to realize that the seemingly mindless wasting of resources, whether material or human, is intrinsic to and inherent in the market itself. Nothing in the market mechanism plans rational usage or harbors resources for the future. Any concern about depletion of resources, pollution, or unemployment is external to the market, and efforts to act on these concerns, whether by government, unions, or consumers, are external to the market and intrude upon its normal operations.

Social Disintegration. Before abandoning this discussion of the disutilities inherent in capitalism, we might also take note of the problem of social disintegration. Ironically, one of the most powerful and important effects of the operations of a market capitalist economy is its tendency to tear apart all stable communities, traditions, and values. I use the word "ironic" because many of the most vocal advocates of market capitalism are precisely those people who most strongly lament the decline of religion, community, and family in American life, and who tend to place the blame for those trends squarely on the shoulders of modern liberals and other egalitarians with their penchant for schemes to interfere with the free and untrammeled operation of the market mechanism. It is precisely the incredible dynamism of the capitalist economy that represents the main force in the destruction of all stable traditions and institutions. How can local communities remain stable and viable when enterprises are free to come and go,[27] when resources are ruthlessly exploited, when families are uprooted to make way for enterprises, or when people are forced to seek jobs in other regions? It is the pace of technological change and the tremendous mobility of private capital in its unending pursuit of gain that are both the power of the market economy and the essence of its destructiveness. How can traditional values and institutions stand the blows of such a dynamic process?[28] The market creates a society of mobility and change, of competition and self-interest. It creates a society of individual self-seekers without obligations or ties. It destroys the ground upon which people might pause to rest. Many individuals, for better or worse, cannot stand the consequences of such a life. This is reflected in distressingly high rates of alcoholism and drug abuse, in divorce, and interpersonal violence. These are the kinds of costs that represent the dark underside of the glittery, gadget-filled capitalist success story.

CONCLUDING REMARKS

This chapter has described the defining elements of capitalism, how these elements relate to each other, and what some of the ramifications of their operations might be for American society. Such descriptions are important for several reasons:

☐ *To demonstrate the ways in which capitalism is distinguished from other economic systems.* While some of the elements we have described can be found in other economic systems, the combination of market-oriented production and a class system based on property are unique to capitalism. Furthermore, while capitalism has been greatly transformed during its three- or four-hundred-year history, class and market remain its defining characteristics.

☐ *To demonstrate the problematic nature of capitalist economies.* We have examined how the class system and the market produce a set of problems that are inescapable; these include inequality, alienation, instability, unemployment, exploitation, irrationality, and wastefulness. While many of these problems can be found in other types of society, it is only in capitalism that they arise out of the very logic of the system. Furthermore, the problematic nature of capitalist production, being intrinsic to social class and market, cannot be changed merely by displacing old piratical entrepreneurs with more humane, Harvard Business School–trained managers. The logic of the economic system forces them to act in very much the same manner.

☐ *To begin to consider the functions of government in the contemporary United States.* One of the most important phenomena that we shall examine is the seemingly inexorable growth in the size and impact of all levels of government in the United States. A substantial part of that growth can be explained by the social havoc wrought by capitalism and by the problems spun off in its development. Government has been forced to intervene in economic and social life because of mass political pressures and because of elite fears of mass instability in the face of the problems caused, paradoxically, by the very successes of capitalism.

This chapter has described a *general* theory of capitalist society relevant to any and all market capitalist systems. As such, it remains at a fairly high level of

The long arm of the consumer economy

abstraction. The next two chapters will describe more carefully the *specific* ways in which capitalism operates in the contemporary United States and how these economic processes affect the possibilities for social justice and democracy. Subsequent chapters will analyze how political institutions and government policy are shaped by American capitalism.

NOTES

1. In the next two chapters, we shall look at our capitalist economy in more concrete terms.
2. Howard Sherman, *Radical Political Economy: Capitalism and Socialism from a Marxist-Humanist Perspective* (New York: Basic Books, 1972).
3. For the story of how corporate investment decisions have substantially deindustrialized the United States, see Barry Bluestone and Bennett Harrison, *The Deindustrialization of America* (New York: Basic Books, 1982).
4. R. H. Tawney, *Equality* (London: Allen and Unwin, 1952), pp. 58, 66.
5. The validity of the concept of surplus value was even recognized by Adam Smith, the greatest theorist of market capitalism: "The value which the workmen add to the material . . . resolves itself . . . into two parts of which the one pays the wages, the other the profits of the employer." *The Wealth of Nations* (Oxford: Clarendon Press, 1976), p. 66.
6. Quoted in Ross Terrill, *R. H. Tawney and His Times* (Cambridge, Mass.: Harvard

University Press, 1967), p. 167. I do not agree that profit is simply the just reward for productive innovation or for abstinence from the immediate use and enjoyment of wealth. For a devastating refutation of these understandings of profit, see Francis Green and Peter Nore, *Economics: An Anti-Textbook* (London: Macmillan, 1977); E. K. Hunt and Jesse Schwartz (eds.), *A Critique of Economic Theory* (London; Penguin, 1972); and Robert Kuttner, *The Economic Illusion* (Boston: Houghton Mifflin, 1984).

7. In those capitalist countries where labor unions are strong, where Social Democratic parties are influential, and where a substantial welfare state exists, the linkage between disposable income and life chances is not as strong as it is in the United States.

8. See his discussion of these issues in C. B. MacPherson, *Democratic Theory: Essays in Retrieval* (London: Clarendon Press, 1973). In most societies that call themselves socialist, different yet equally serious obstacles to the development of human capacities exist (see chapter 15). For the best comparison of capitalist and socialist societies, see Branko Horvat, *The Political Economy of Socialism* (Armonk, N.Y.: M. E. Sharpe, 1982).

9. See the discussion of the history of work organization and the accelerating pace of the division of labor in Harry Braverman, *Labor and Monopoly Capital* (New York: Monthly Review Press, 1974). Also see Michael Burawoy, *The Politics of Production* (London: Verso, 1985); and Dan Clawson, *Bureaucracy and the Labor Process* (New York: Monthly Review Press, 1980).

10. Karl Marx referred to this separation between the human essence and reality of most people's everyday life as *alienation*. For the best introductions to Marx's concept of alienation, see Shlomo Avineri, *The Social and Political Thought of Karl Marx* (New York: Cambridge University Press, 1968); Erich Fromm, *Marx's Conception of Man* (New York: Ungar, 1961); and Bertall Ollman, *Alienation: Marx's Conception of Man in Capitalist Society* (New York: Cambridge University Press, 1971). Also see Horvat, *The Political Economy of Socialism.*

11. Paul Blumberg, *Industrial Democracy: The Sociology of Participation* (New York: Schocken Books, 1969); Melvin Kohn and Carmi Schooler, *Work and Personality* (Norwood, N.J.: Aldex Publishing, 1983); Arthur Kornhauser, *The Mental Health of the Industrial Worker* (New York: Wiley, 1965); H. L. Sheppard and N. Q. Herrick, *Where Have All the Robots Gone? Worker Dissatisfaction in the Seventies* (New York: Free Press, 1972); Ronald Mason, *Participatory and Workplace Democracy* (Carbondale, Ill.: University of Southern Illinois Press, 1982); Studs Terkel, *Working* (New York: Pantheon, 1972). For provocative introductions to alternative forms of work organization, see Martin Carnoy and Derek Shearer, *Economic Democracy* (New York: M. E. Sharpe, 1980); Robert Dahl, *A Preface to Economic Democracy* (Berkeley: University of California Press, 1985); Christopher Gunn, *Worker's Self-Management in the United States* (Ithaca: Cornell University Press, 1984); and Daniel Zwerdling, *Workplace Democracy* (New York: Harper & Row, Colophon Books, 1980).

12. Terkel, *Working*, p. xxxii.

13. Adam Smith, *The Wealth of Nations* (Oxford: Clarendon, 1976), pp. 781–782.

14. Given the general misunderstanding of this fundamental concept, social class, an important qualification is in order. My presentation of capitalist society as composed of two opposed classes is meant as a model. As with any scientific model, this one does not claim absolute fidelity to all of the details of any particular society. All scientific models are simplifications of reality that advance our understanding by extracting and highlighting the essentials and placing less important matters in the background. I most certainly understand that the actual class structure of the United

States is infinitely more complex. I shall explore these issues more closely in the next chapter.

15. For a compelling and poignant description of the impact of the American presence on traditional Vietnamese society, see Frances FitzGerald, *Fire in the Lake* (New York: Vintage, 1973). One might also view the Academy Award-winning documentary film "Hearts and Minds."

16. Karl Polanyi, *The Great Transformation* (Boston; Beacon Press, 1957), pp. 33, 163.

17. An economic boom driven by deficit spending and created by a self-avowed fiscal conservative is, of course, one of history's many delicious ironies.

18. To be sure, inflation is also the product of natural and artificial scarcities, of massive government deficits, and of the practice of "administered pricing," whereby giant corporate enterprises largely set their own market prices (see chapter 7).

19. Economic fluctuations occur in socialist countries, but they are distinctly different. Not only are they less severe, but they are characterized by alterations in the rates of real growth, not by absolute declines in output and employment. See Sherman, *Radical Political Economy*, Ch. 17.

20. For elaboration of this point, see Horvat, *The Political Economy of Socialism*, pp. 192–198; and Robert Magaziner and Robert Reich, *Minding America's Business* (New York: Harcourt Brace Jovanovich, 1982).

21. While somewhat dated, the best discussion of these issues continues to be K. William Kapp, *The Social Costs of Private Enterprise* (New York: Schocken Books, 1971).

22. Quoted in William Serrin, *The Company and the Union* (New York: Vintage, 1974).

23. A study by Brad Snell for the U.S. Senate Judiciary Committee (1974) reported that General Motors, Standard Oil, and Firestone Tire had long been involved in a conscious strategy to buy and ruin urban rail systems in order to create a market for buses, trucks, and automobiles.

24. Barry Commoner, *The Closing Circle* (New York: Knopf, 1971), pp. 143–145.

25. Ibid., p. 145. During this period, Commoner reports, there were the following increases in production: nonreturnable soda bottles, up 52,000 percent; synthetic fibers, up 5,980 percent; mercury for chlorine detergents, up 3,930 percent; and so on.

26. André Gorz, *A Strategy for Labor* (Boston: Beacon Press, 1967), p. 79.

27. For the story of mobile capital and community decline, see Bluestone and Harrison, *The Deindustrialization of America.*

28. Note the rapid decline in the number of family farms in the United States under the engine of farm consolidation into corporate farms. *The New York Times* (August 4, 1987) reports that the top 1.2 percent of corporate farms accounted for 33 percent of *all* agricultural production and 55.3 percent of *all* farm profits in 1987.

SUGGESTIONS FOR FURTHER READING

Harry Braverman. LABOR AND MONOPOLY CAPITAL. *New York: Monthly Review Press, 1974.* A brilliant analysis of transformations in the nature of work.

Milton Friedman. CAPITALISM AND FREEDOM. *Chicago: University of Chicago Press, 1962.* The leading and most influential defense of the competitive free market system by the Nobel Prize–winning economist.

Robert Heilbroner. THE NATURE AND LOGIC OF CAPITALISM. *New York: Norton, 1985.* A concise yet brilliant evocation of the inner dynamics and structures of capitalism.

Branko Horvat. THE POLITICAL ECONOMY OF SOCIALISM. *Armonk, N.Y.: M. E. Sharpe, Inc., 1982.*

K. William Kapp. THE SOCIAL COSTS OF PRIVATE ENTERPRISE. *New York: Schocken Books,*
   1971. A close look at the dark underside of free enterprise.
Robert Kuttner. THE ECONOMIC ILLUSION. *Boston: Houghton Mifflin, 1984.* In this book,
   the old saw is put to rest that a basic contradiction always exists between equality and
   economic efficiency.
Adam Smith. THE WEALTH OF NATIONS. *Oxford: Clarendon, 1976.* The founding text of
   market capitalism remains must reading.
R. H. Tawney. THE ACQUISITIVE SOCIETY. *New York: Harcourt, Brace & World, 1920.*
   A classic and still compelling description of the behavioral and attitudinal attributes
   of capitalism.
Eric Wolf. EUROPE AND THE PEOPLE WITHOUT HISTORY. *Berkeley: University of Califor-*
   nia Press, 1982. The best single work charting the rise of the world capitalist system.

Appendix:
The Constitution
of the United States

We the People of the United States, in Order to form a more perfect Union, establish Justice, insure domestic Tranquility, provide for the common defense, promote the general Welfare, and secure the Blessings of Liberty to ourselves and our Posterity, do ordain and establish this Constitution for the United States of America.

Article I

Section 1. All legislative Powers herein granted shall be vested in a Congress of the United States, which shall consist of a Senate and House of Representatives.

Section 2. The House of Representatives shall be composed of Members chosen every second Year by the People of the several States, and the Electors in each State shall have the Qualifications requisite for Electors of the most numerous Branch of the State Legislature.

No Person shall be a Representative who shall not have attained to the Age of twenty-five Years, and been seven Years A Citizen of the United States, and who shall not, when elected, be an Inhabitant of that State in which he shall be chosen.

Representatives and direct Taxes shall be apportioned among the several States which may be included within this Union, according to their respective Numbers, which shall be determined by adding to the whole Number of free Persons, including those bound to Service for a Term of Years, and excluding Indians not taxed, three fifths of all other Persons. The actual Enumeration shall be made within three Years after the first Meeting of the Congress of the United States, and within every subsequent Term of ten Years, in such Manner as they shall by Law direct. The Number of Representatives shall not exceed one for every thirty Thousand, but each State shall have at Least one Representative; and until such enumeration shall be made, the State of New Hampshire shall be entitled to chuse three, Massachusetts eight, Rhode-Island and Providence Plantations one, Connecticut five, New York six, New Jersey four, Pennsylvania eight, Delaware one, Maryland six, Virginia ten, North Carolina five, South Carolina five, and Georgia three.

When vacancies happen in the Representation from any State, the Executive Authority thereof shall issue Writs of Election to fill such Vacancies.

The House of Representatives shall chuse their Speaker and other Officers; and shall have the sole Power of Impeachment.

Section 3. The Senate of the United States shall be composed of two Senators from each State, chosen by the Legislature thereof, for six Years; and each Senator shall have one Vote.

Immediately after they shall be assembled in Consequence of the first Election, they shall be divided as equally as may be into three Classes. The Seats of the Senators of the first Class shall be vacated at the Expiration of the second Year, of the second Class at the Expiration of the fourth Year, and of the third Class at the Expiration of the sixth Year, so that one third may be chosen every second Year; and if Vacancies happen by Resignation, or otherwise, during the Recess of the Legislature of any State, the Executive thereof may make temporary Appointments until the next Meeting of the Legislature, which shall then fill such Vacancies.

No Person shall be a Senator who shall not have attained to the Age of thirty Years, and been nine Years a Citizen of the United States, and who shall not, when elected, be an Inhabitant of the State for which he shall be chosen.

The Vice President of the United States shall be President of the Senate, but shall have no Vote, unless they be equally divided.

The Senate shall chuse their other Officers, and also a President pro tempore, in the absence of the Vice President, or when he shall exercise the Office of President of the United States.

The Senate shall have the sole Power to try all Impeachments. When sitting for that Purpose, they shall be on Oath or Affirmation. When the President of the United States is tried, the Chief Justice shall preside: And no Person shall be convicted without the Concurrence of two thirds of the Members present.

Judgment in Cases of Impeachment shall not extend further than to removal from Office, and disqualification to hold and enjoy any Office of honor, Trust, or Profit under the United States: but the Party convicted shall nevertheless be liable and subject to Indictment, Trial, Judgment and Punishment, according to Law.

Section 4. The Times, Places and Manner of holding Elections for Senators and Representatives, shall be prescribed in each State by the Legislature thereof; but the Congress may at any time by Law make or alter such Regulations, except as to the Places of chusing Senators.

The Congress shall assemble at least once in every Year, and such Meeting shall be on the first Monday in December, unless they shall by Law appoint a different Day.

Section 5. Each House shall be the judge of the Elections, Returns and Qualifications of its own Members, and a Majority of such shall constitute a Quorum to do Business; but a smaller Number may adjourn from day to day, and may be authorized to compel the Attendance of absent Members, in such Manner, and under such Penalties, as each House may provide.

Each House may determine the Rules of its Proceedings, punish its Members for disorderly Behaviour, and, with the Concurrence of two thirds, expel a Member.

Each House shall keep a Journal of its Proceedings, and from time to time publish the same, excepting such Parts as may in their Judgment require Secrecy; and the Yeas and Nays of the Members of either House on any question shall, at the Desire of one fifth of those Present, be entered on the Journal.

Neither House, during the Session of Congress, shall, without the Consent of the other, adjourn for more than three days, nor to any other Place than that in which the two Houses shall be sitting.

Section 6. The Senators and Representatives shall receive a Compensation for their Services, to be ascertained by Law, and paid out of the Treasury of the United States. They shall in all Cases, except Treason, Felony and Breach of the Peace, be privileged from Arrest during their Attendance at the Session of their respective Houses, and in going to and returning from the same; and for any Speech or Debate in either House, they shall not be questioned in any other place.

No Senator or Representative shall, during the Time for which he was elected, be appointed to any civil Office under the Authority of the United States, which shall have been created, or the Emoluments whereof shall have been encreased during such time; and no Person holding any Office under the United States, shall be a Member of either House during his Continuance in Office.

Section 7. All bills for raising Revenue shall originate in the House of Representatives; but the Senate may propose or concur with Amendments as on other Bills.

Every Bill which shall have passed the House of Representatives and the Senate, shall, before it become a Law, be presented to the President of the United States; If he approve he shall sign it, but if not he shall return it, with his Objections to that House in which it shall have originated, who shall enter the Objections at large on their Journal, and proceed to reconsider it. If after such Reconsideration two thirds of that House shall agree to pass the Bill, it shall be sent, together with the Objections, to the other House, by which it shall likewise be reconsidered, and if approved by two thirds of that House, it shall become a Law. But in all such Cases the Votes of both Houses shall be determined by Yeas and Nays, and the Names of the Persons voting for and against the Bill shall be entered on the Journal of each House respectively. If any Bill shall not be returned by the President within ten Days (Sundays excepted) after it shall have been presented to him, the Same shall be a Law, in like Manner as if he had signed it, unless the Congress by their Adjournment prevent its Return, in which Case it shall not be a Law.

Every Order, Resolution, or Vote to which the Concurrence of the Senate and House of Representatives may be necessary (except on a question of Adjournment) shall be presented to the President of the United States; and before the Same shall take Effect, shall be approved by him, or being disapproved by him, shall be repassed by two thirds of the Senate and House of Representatives, according to the Rules and Limitations prescribed in the Case of a Bill.

Section 8. The Congress shall have Power To lay and collect Taxes, Duties, Imposts and Excises, to pay the Debts and provide for the common Defense and general Welfare of the United States; but all Duties, Imposts and Excises shall be uniform throughout the United States;

To borrow Money on the credit of the United States;

To regulate Commerce with foreign Nations, and among the several States, and with the Indian Tribes;

To establish an uniform Rule of Naturalization, and uniform Laws on the subject of Bankruptcies throughout the United States;

To coin Money, regulate the Value thereof, and of foreign Coin, and fix the Standard of Weights and Measures;

To provide for the Punishment of counterfeiting the Securities and current Coin of the United States;

To Establish Post Offices and post Roads;

To promote the Progress of Science and useful Arts, by securing for limited Times to Authors and Inventors the exclusive Right to their respective Writings and Discoveries;

To constitute Tribunals inferior to the Supreme Court;

To define and punish Piracies and Felonies committed on the high seas, and Offenses against the Law of Nations;

To declare War, grant Letters of Marque and Reprisal, and make Rules concerning Captures on Land and Water;

To raise and support Armies, but no Appropriation of Money to that Use shall be for a longer Term than two Years;

To provide and maintain a Navy;

To make Rules for the Government and Regulation of the land and naval Forces;

To provide for calling forth the Militia to execute the Laws of the Union, suppress Insurrections and repel Invasions;

To provide for organizing, arming, and disciplining, the Militia, and for governing such Part of them as may be employed in the Service of the United States, reserving to the States respectively, the Appointment of the Officers, and the Authority of training the Militia according to the discipline prescribed by Congress;

To exercise exclusive Legislation in all Cases whatsoever, over such District (not exceeding ten Miles square) as may, by Cession of particular States, and the Acceptance of Congress, become the Seat of the Government of the United States, and to exercise like Authority over all Places purchased by the Consent of the Legislature of the State in which the Same shall be, for the Erection of Forts, Magazines, Arsenals, dock-Yards, and other needful Buildings;—And

To make all Laws which shall be necessary and proper for carrying into Execution the foregoing Powers, and all other Powers vested by this Constitution in the Government of the United States, or in any Department or Officer thereof.

Section 9. The Migration or Importation of such Persons as any of the States now existing shall think proper to admit, shall not be prohibited by the Congress prior to the Year one thousand eight hundred and eight, but a Tax or duty may be imposed on such Importation, not exceeding ten dollars for each Person.

The Privilege of the Writ of Habeas Corpus shall not be suspended, unless when in Cases of Rebellion or Invasion the public Safety may require it.

No Bill of Attainder or ex post factor Law shall be passed.

No Capitation, or other direct, Tax shall be laid, unless in Proportion to the Census or Enumeration herein before directed to be taken.

No Tax or Duty shall be laid on Articles exported from any State.

No Preference shall be given by any Regulation of Commerce or Revenue to the Ports of one State over those of another; nor shall Vessels bound to, or from, one State, be obliged to enter, clear, or pay Duties in another.

No Money shall be drawn from the Treasury, but in Consequence of Appropriations made by Law; and a regular Statement and Account of the Receipts and Expenditures of all public Money shall be published from time to time.

No title of Nobility shall be granted by the United States: And no Person holding any Office of Profit or Trust under them, shall, without the Consent of the Congress, accept of any present, Emolument, Office, or Title, or any kind whatever, from any King, Prince, or foreign State.

Section 10. No State shall enter into any Treaty, Alliance, or Confederation; grant Letters of Marque and Reprisal; coin Money; emit Bills of Credit; make any Thing but gold and silver Coin a Tender in Payment of Debts; pass any Bill of Attainder, ex post facto Law, or Law impairing the Obligation of Contracts, or Grant any Title of Nobility.

No State shall, without the Consent of the Congress, lay any Imposts or Duties on Imports or Exports, except what may be absolutely necessary for exercising its inspection Laws: and the net Produce of all Duties and Imposts, laid by any State on Imports or Exports shall be for the Use of the Treasury of the United States; and all such Laws shall be subject to the Revision and Control of the Congress.

No State shall, without the Consent of Congress, lay any duty of Tonnage, keep Troops, or Ships of War in time of Peace, enter into any Agreement or Compact with another State, or with a foreign Power, or engage in War, unless actually invaded, or in such imminent Danger as will not admit of delay.

Article II

Section 1. The executive Power shall be vested in a President of the United States of America. He shall hold his Office during the Term of four Years, and, together with the Vice President, chosen for the same Term be elected, as follows:

Each state shall appoint, in such Manner as the Legislature thereof may direct, a Number of Electors, equal to the whole Number of Senators and Representatives to which the State may be entitled in the Congress but no Senator or Representative, or Person holding an Office of Trust or Profit under the United States, shall be appointed an Elector.

The Electors shall meet in their respective States, and vote by Ballot for two Persons, of whom one at least shall not be an Inhabitant of the same State with themselves. And they shall make a List of all the Persons voted for, and of the Number of Votes for each; which List they shall sign and certify, and transmit sealed to the Seat of the Government of the United States, directed to the President of the Senate. The President of the Senate shall, in the Presence of the Senate and House of Representatives, open all the Certificates, and the Votes shall then be counted. The Person having the greatest Number of Votes shall be the President, if such Number be a Majority of the whole Number of Electors appointed; and if there be more than one who have such Majority, and have an equal Number of Votes, then the House of Representatives shall immediately chuse by Ballot one of them for President; and if no Person have a Majority, then from the five highest on the List the said House shall in like Manner chuse the President. But in chusing the President, the Votes shall be taken by States, the Representation from each State having one Vote; A quorum for this Purpose shall consist of a Member or Members from two thirds of the States, and a Majority of all the States shall be necessary to a Choice. In every Case, after the Choice of the President, the Person having the greatest Number of Votes of the Electors shall be the Vice President. But if there should remain two or more who have equal votes, the Senate shall chuse from them by Ballot the Vice President.

The Congress may determine the Time of chusing the Electors, and the Day on which they shall give their Votes; which Day shall be the same throughout the United States.

No Person except a natural born Citizen, or a Citizen of the United States, at the time of the Adoption of this Constitution, shall be eligible to the Office of President; neither shall any Person be eligible to that Office who shall not have attained to the Age of thirty-five Years, and been fourteen years a Resident within the United States.

In Case of the Removal of the President from Office, or of his Death, Resignation, or Inability to discharge the Powers and Duties of the said Office, the Same shall devolve on the Vice President, and the Congress may by Law provide for the Case of Removal, Death, Resignation or Inability, both of the President and Vice President, declaring what Officer shall then act as President, and such Officer shall act accordingly, until the Disability be removed, or a President shall be elected.

The President shall, at stated Times, receive for his Services, a Compensation which shall neither be increased nor diminished during the Period for which he shall have been elected, and he shall not receive within that Period any other Emolument from the United States, or any of them.

Before he enters on the Execution of his Office, he shall take the following Oath or Affirmation:—"I do solemnly swear (or affirm) that I will faithfully execute the Office of President of the United States, and will to the best of my Ability, preserve, protect, and defend the Constitution of the United States."

Section 2. The President shall be Commander in Chief of the Army and Navy of the United States, and of the Militia of the several States, when called into the actual service of the United States; he may require the Opinion, in writing, of the principal Officer in each of the Executive Departments, upon any Subject relating to the Duties of their respective Offices, and he shall have Power to grant Reprieves and Pardons for Offenses against the United States, except in Cases of Impeachment.

He shall have Power, by and with the Advice and Consent of the Senate, to make Treaties, provided two thirds of the Senators present concur; and he shall nominate, and by and with the Advice and Consent of the Senate, shall appoint Ambassadors, other public Ministers and Consuls, Judges of the supreme Court, and all other Officers of the United States, whose Appointments are not herein otherwise provided for, and which shall be established by Law: but the Congress may by Law vest the Appointment of such inferior Officers, as they think proper, in the President alone, in the Courts of Law, or in the Heads of Departments.

The President shall have Power to fill up all Vacancies that may happen during the Recess of the Senate, by granting Commissions which shall expire at the End of their next Session.

Section 3. He shall from time to time give to the Congress Information of the State of the Union, and recommend to their Consideration such Measures as he shall judge necessary and expedient; he may, on extraordinary Occasions, convene both Houses, or either of them, and in Case of Disagreement between them, with Respect to the Time of Adjournment, he may adjourn them to such Time as he shall think proper; he shall receive Ambassadors and other public Ministers, he shall take Care that the Laws be faithfully executed, and shall Commission all the Officers of the United States.

Section 4. The President, Vice President, and all civil Officers of the United States shall be removed from Office on Impeachment for, and Conviction of Treason, Bribery, or other high Crimes and Misdemeanors.

Article III

Section 1. The judicial Power of the United States, shall be vested in one supreme Court and in such inferior Courts as the Congress may from time to time ordain and establish. The Judges, both of the supreme and inferior Courts, shall hold their Offices during good Behavior, and shall, at stated Times, receive for their Services, a Compensation, which shall not be diminished during their Continuance in Office.

Section 2. The judicial Power shall extend to all Cases, in Law and Equity, arising under this Constitution, the Laws of the United States, and Treaties made, or which shall be made, under their Authority;—to all Cases affecting

Ambassadors, other public Ministers and Consuls;—to all Cases of admiralty and maritime Jurisdiction;—to Controversies to which the United States shall be a Party;—to Controversies between two or more States;—between a State and Citizens of another State;—between Citizens of different States;—between Citizens of the same State claiming Lands under Grants of different States, and between a State or the Citizens thereof, and foreign States, Citizens, or Subjects.

In all cases affecting Ambassadors, other public Ministers and Consuls, and those in which a State shall be a Party, the supreme Court shall have original Jurisdiction. In all the other Cases before mentioned, the supreme Court shall have appellate Jurisdiction, both as to Law and Fact, with such Exceptions, and under such Regulations as the Congress shall make.

The Trial of all Crimes, except in Cases of Impeachment, shall be by Jury; and such Trial shall be held in the State where the said Crimes shall have been committed; but when not committed within any State, the Trial shall be at such Place or Places as the Congress may by Law have directed.

Section 3. Treason against the United States, shall consist only in levying War against them, or in adhering to their Enemies, giving them Aid and Comfort. No person shall be convicted of Treason unless on the Testimony of two Witnesses to the same overt Act, or on Confession in open Court.

The Congress shall have Power to declare the Punishment of Treason, but no Attainder of Treason shall work Corruption of Blood, or Forfeiture except during the Life of the Person attained.

Article IV

Section 1. Full Faith and Credit shall be given in each State to the public Acts, Records, and Judicial Proceedings of every other State. And the Congress may by general Laws prescribe the Manner in which such Acts, Records, and Proceedings shall be proved, and the Effect thereof.

Section 2. The Citizens of each State shall be entitled to all Privileges and Immunities of Citizens in the several States.

A person charged in any State with Treason, Felony, or other Crime, who shall flee from Justice, and be found in another State, shall on Demand of the executive Authority of the State from which he fled, he delivered up, to be removed to the State having Jurisdiction of the Crime.

No Person held to Service or Labour in one State, under the Laws thereof, escaping into another, shall, in Consequence of any Law or Regulation therein, be discharged from such Service or Labour, but shall be delivered up on Claim of the Party to whom such Service or Labour may be due.

Section 3. New States may be admitted by the Congress into this Union; but no new State shall be formed or erected within the Jurisdiction of any other State; nor any State be formed by the Junction of two or more States, or parts of States, without the Consent of the Legislatures of the States concerned as well as of the Congress.

The Congress shall have Power to dispose of and make all needful Rules and Regulations respecting the Territory or other Property belonging to the United States; and nothing in this Constitution shall be so construed as to Prejudice any Claims of the United States, or of any particular State.

Section 4. The United States shall guarantee to every State in this Union a Republican Form of Government, and shall protect each of them against Invasion; and on Application of the Legislature, or of the Executive (when the Legislature cannot be convened) against domestic Violence.

Article V

The Congress, whenever two thirds of both Houses shall deem it necessary, shall propose Amendments to this Constitution, or, on the Application of the Legislatures of two thirds of the several States, shall call a Convention for proposing Amendments, which, in either Case, shall be valid to all Intents and Purposes, as Part of this Constitution, when ratified by the Legislatures of three fourths of the several States, or by Conventions in three fourths thereof, as the one or the other Mode of Ratification may be proposed by the Congress; Provided that no Amendment which may be made prior to the Year One thousand eight hundred and eight shall in any Manner affect the first and fourth Clauses in the Ninth Section of the first Article; and that no State, without its Consent, shall be deprived of its equal Suffrage in the Senate.

Article VI

All Debts contracted and Engagements entered into, before the Adoption of this Constitution, shall be as valid against the United States under this Constitution, as under the Confederation.

This Constitution, and the Laws of the United States which shall be made in Pursuance thereof; and all Treaties made, or which shall be made, under the Authority of the United States, shall be the supreme Law of the Land; and the Judges in every State shall be bound thereby, any Thing in the Constitution or Laws of any State to the Contrary notwithstanding.

The Senators and Representatives before mentioned, and the Members of the several State Legislatures, and all executive and judicial Officers, both of the United States and of the several States, shall be bound by Oath or Affirmation to support this Constitution; but no religious Test shall ever be required as a Qualification to any Office or public Trust under the United States.

Article VII

The Ratification of the Conventions of nine States shall be sufficient for the Establishment of this Constitution between the States so ratifying the Same.

Done in Convention by the Unanimous Consent of the States present the Seventeenth Day of September in the Year of our Lord one thousand seven hundred and eighty seven and of the Independence of the United States of America the twelfth. In witness whereof We have hereunto subscribed our Names.

Articles in addition to, and amendment of, the Constitution of the United States of America, proposed by Congress, and ratified by the several states, pursuant to the fifth article of the original Constitution.

Amendment I

[Ratification of the first ten amendments was completed December 15, 1791.] Congress shall make no law respecting an establishment of religion, or prohibiting the free exercise thereof; or abridging the freedom of speech, or of the press; or the right of the people peaceably to assemble, and to petition the Government for a redress of grievances.

Amendment II

A well regulated Militia, being necessary to the security of a free State, the right of the people to keep and bear Arms, shall not be infringed.

Amendment III

No Soldier shall, in time of peace, be quartered in any house, without the consent of the Owner, nor in time of war, but in a manner to be prescribed by law.

Amendment IV

The right of the people to be sure in their persons, houses, papers, and effects, against unreasonable searches and seizures, shall not be violated, and no Warrants shall issue, but upon probable cause, supported by Oath or affirmation, and particularly describing the place to be searched, and the persons or things to be seized.

Amendment V

No person shall be held to answer for a capital, or other infamous crime, unless on a presentment or indictment of a Grand Jury, except in cases arising in the land or naval forces, or in the Militia, when in actual service in time of War or public danger; nor shall any person be subject for the same offence to be twice put in jeopardy of life and limb; nor shall be compelled in any capital crime case to be witness against himself, nor be deprived of life, liberty, or property, without due process of law; nor shall private property be taken for public use, without just compensation.

Amendment VI

In all criminal prosecutions, the accused shall enjoy the right to a speedy and public trial, by an impartial jury of the State and district wherein the crime shall have been committed, which district shall have been previously ascertained by law, and to be informed of the nature and cause of the accusation; to be confronted with the witness against him; to have compulsory process for obtaining witness in his favor, and to have the Assistance of Counsel for his defence.

Amendment VII

In Suits at common law, where the value in controversy shall exceed twenty dollars, the right of trial by jury shall be preserved, and no fact tried by jury, shall be otherwise re-examined in any Court of the United States, than according to the rules of the common law.

Amendment VIII

Excessive bail shall not be required, nor excessive fines imposed, nor cruel and unusual punishments inflicted.

Amendment IX

The enumeration in the Constitution, of certain rights, shall not be construed to deny or disparage others retained by the people.

Amendment X

The powers not delegated to the United States by the Constitution, nor prohibited by it to the States, are reserved to the States respectively, or to the people.

Amendment XI

[January 8, 1798]

The Judicial power of the United States shall not be construed to extend to any suit in law or equity, commenced or prosecuted against one of the United States by Citizens of another State, or by Citizens or subjects of any Foreign State.

Amendment XII

[September 25, 1804]

The Electors shall meet in their respective states and vote by ballot for President and Vice President, one of whom, at least, shall not be an inhabitant of the same state with themselves; they shall name in their ballots the person voted for as President, and in distinct ballots the person voted for as Vice President, and they shall make distinct lists of all persons voted for as President, and of all persons voted for as Vice President, and of the number of votes for each, which lists they shall sign and certify, and transmit sealed to the seat of the government of the United States, directed to the President of the Senate;—The President of the Senate shall, in the presence of Senate and House of Representatives, open all the certificates and the votes shall then be counted;—The person having the greatest number of votes for President, shall be the President, if such number be a majority of the whole number of Electors appointed; and if no person have such majority, then from the persons having the highest numbers not exceeding three on the list of those voted for as President, the House of Representatives shall choose immediately, by ballot, the President. But in choosing the President, the votes shall be taken by states, the representation from each state having one vote; a quorum for this purpose shall consist of a member or members from two-thirds of the states, and a majority of all the states shall be necessary to a choice. And if the states, and a majority of all the states shall be necessary to a choice. And if the House of Representatives shall not choose a President whenever the right of choice shall devolve upon them, before the fourth day of March next following, then the Vice President shall act as President, as in the case of the death or other constitutional disability of the President.—The person having the greatest number of votes as Vice President shall be the Vice President, if such number be a majority of the whole number of Electors appointed, and if no person have a majority, then from the two highest numbers on the list, the Senate shall choose the Vice President; a quorum for the purpose shall consist of two-thirds of the whole number of Senators, and a majority of the whole number shall be necessary to a choice. But no person constitutionally ineligible to the office of President shall be eligible to that of Vice President of the United States.

Amendment XIII
[December 18, 1865]

Section 1. Neither slavery nor involuntary servitude, except as a punishment for crime whereof the party shall have been duly convicted, shall exist within the United States, or any place subject to their jurisdiction.

Section 2. Congress shall have power to enforce this article by appropriate legislation.

Amendment XIV
[July 28, 1869]

Section 1. All persons born or naturalized in the United States, and subject to the jurisdiction thereof, are citizens of the United States and of the State wherein they reside. No State shall make or enforce any law which shall abridge the privileges or immunities of citizens of the United States; nor shall any State deprive any person of life, liberty, or property, without due process of law; nor deny to any person within its jurisdiction the equal protection of the laws.

Section 2. Representatives shall be apportioned among the several States according to their respective numbers, counting the whole number of persons in each State, excluding Indians not taxed. But when the right to vote at any election for the choice of electors for President and Vice President of the United States, Representatives in Congress, the Executive and Judicial officers of a State, or the members of the Legislature thereof, is denied to any of the male inhabitants of such State, being twenty-one years of age, and citizens of the United States, or in any way abridged, except for participation in rebellion, or other crime, the basis of representation therein shall be reduced in the proportion which the number of such male citizens shall bear to the whole number of male citizens twenty-one years of age in such State.

Section 3. No person shall be a Senator or Representative in Congress, or elector of President and Vice President, or hold any office, civil or military, under the United States, or under any State, who, having previously taken an oath, as a member of Congress, or as an officer of the United States, or as a member of any

State legislature, or as an executive or judicial officer of any State, to support the Constitution of the United States, shall have engaged in insurrection or rebellion against the same, or given aid or comfort to the enemies thereof. But Congress may by a vote of two-thirds of each House, remove such disability.

Section 4.   The validity of the public debt of the United States, authorized by law, including debts incurred for payment of pensions and bounties for services in suppressing insurrection or rebellion, shall not be questioned. But neither the United States nor any State shall assume or pay any debt or obligation incurred in aid of insurrection or rebellion against the United States, or any claim for the loss or emancipation of any slave; but all such debts, obligations, and claims shall be held illegal and void.

Section 5.   The Congress shall have power to enforce, by appropriate legislation, the provisions of this article.

Amendment XV
[March 30, 1870]

Section 1.   The right of citizens of the United States to vote shall not be denied or abridged by the United States or by any State on account of race, color, or previous condition of servitude.

Section 2.   The Congress shall have the power to enforce this article by appropriate legislation.

Amendment XVI
[February 25, 1913]
The Congress shall have power to lay and collect taxes on incomes, from whatever source derived, without apportionment among the several States, and without regard to any census or enumeration.

Amendment XVII
[May 31, 1913]
The Senate of the United States shall be composed of two Senators from each State, elected by the people thereof, for six years; and each Senator shall have one vote. The electors in each State shall have the qualifications requisite for electors of the most numerous branch of the State legislatures.

When vacancies happen in the representation of any State in the Senate, the executive authority of such State shall issue writs of election to fill such vacancies: *Provided,* That the legislature of any State may empower the executive thereof to make temporary appointments until the people fill the vacancies by election as the legislature may direct.

This amendment shall not be so construed as to affect the election or term of any Senator chosen before it becomes valid as part of the Constitution.

Amendment XVIII
[January 29, 1919]

Section 1. After one year from the ratification of this article the manufacture, sale, or transportation of intoxicating liquors within, the importation therefore into, or the exportation thereof from the United States and all territory subject to the jurisdiction thereof for beverage purposes is hereby prohibited.

Section 2. The Congress and the several States shall have concurrent power to enforce this article by appropriate legislation.

Section 3. This article shall be inoperative unless it shall have been ratified as an amendment to the Constitution by the legislatures of the several States, as provided in the Constitution, within seven years from the date of the submission hereof to the States by the Congress.

Amendment XIX
[August 26, 1920]
The right of citizens of the United States to vote shall not be denied or abridged by the United States or by any State on account of sex.
    Congress shall have power to enforce this article by appropriate legislation.

Amendment XX
[February 6, 1933]

Section 1. The terms of the President and Vice President shall end at noon on the 20th day of January, and the terms of Senators and Representatives at noon on the 3rd day of January, of the years in which such terms would have ended if this article had not been ratified; and the terms of their successors shall then begin.

Section 2. The Congress shall assemble at least once in every year, and such meeting shall begin at noon on the 3rd day of January, unless they shall by law appoint a different day.

Section 3. If, at the time fixed for the beginning of the term of the President, the President elect shall have died, the Vice President elect shall become President. If a President shall not have been chosen before the time fixed for the beginning of his term, or if the President elect shall have failed to qualify, then the Vice President elect shall act as President until a President shall have qualified; and the Congress may by law provide for the case wherein neither a President elect nor a Vice President elect shall have qualified, declaring who shall then act as President, or the manner in which one who is to act shall be selected, and such person shall act accordingly until a President or Vice President shall have qualified.

Section 4. The Congress may by law provide for the case of the death of any of the persons from whom the House of Representatives may choose a President whenever the right of choice shall devolve upon them, and for the case of the death of any of the persons from whom the Senate may choose a Vice President whenever the right of choice shall have devolved upon them.

Section 5. Sections 1 and 2 shall take effect on the 15th day of October following the ratification of this article.

Section 6. This article shall be inoperative unless it shall have been ratified as an amendment to the Constitution by the legislatures of three-fourths of the several States within seven years from the date of its submission.

Amendment XXI
[December 5, 1933]

Section 1. The eighteenth article of amendment to the Constitution of the United States is hereby repealed.

Section 2. The transportation or importation into any State, Territory, or possession of the United States for delivery or use therein of intoxicating liquors, in violation of the laws thereof, is hereby prohibited.

Section 3. This article shall be inoperative unless it shall have been ratified as an amendment to the Constitution by conventions in the several States, as provided in the Constitution, within seven years from the date of the submission hereof to the States by the Congress.

Amendment XXII
[February 26, 1951]

Section 1. No person shall be elected to the office of the President more than twice, and no person who has held the office of President, or acted as President, for more than two years of a term to which some other person was elected President shall be elected to the office of President more than once. But this Article shall not apply to any person holding the office of President when this Article was proposed by the Congress, and shall not prevent any person who may be holding the office of President, or acting as President, during the term within which this Article becomes operative from holding the office of President or acting as President during the remainder of such term.

Section 2. This article shall be inoperative unless it shall have been ratified as an amendment to the Constitution by the legislatures of three fourths of the several States within seven years from the date of its submission to the States by the Congress.

Amendment XXIII
[March 29, 1961]

Section 1. The District constituting the seat of Government of the United States shall appoint in such manner as the Congress may direct:

A number of electors of President and Vice President equal to the whole number of Senators and Representatives in Congress to which the District would be entitled if it were a State, but in no event more than the least populous State; they shall be in addition to those appointed by the States, but they shall be considered, for the purposes of the election of President and Vice President, to be electors appointed by a State; and they shall meet in the District and perform such duties as provided by the twelfth article of amendment.

Section 2. The Congress shall have power to enforce this article by appropriate legislation.

Amendment XXIV
[January 23, 1964]

Section 1. The right of citizens of the United States to vote in any primary or other election for President or Vice President, for electors for President or Vice President, or for Senator or Representative in Congress, shall not be denied or abridged by the United States or any state by reason of failure to pay any poll tax or other tax.

Section 2. The Congress shall have the power to enforce this article by appropriate legislation.

Amendment XXV
[February 19, 1967]

Section 1. In case of the removal of the President from office or of his death or resignation, the Vice President shall become President.

Section 2. Whenever there is a vacancy in the office of the Vice President, the President shall nominate a Vice President who shall take office upon confirmation by a majority vote of both Houses of Congress.

Section 3. Whenever the President transmits to the President pro tempore of the Senate and the Speaker of the House of Representatives his written declaration that he is unable to discharge the powers and duties of his office, and until he transmits to them a written declaration to the contrary, such powers and duties shall be discharged by the Vice President as Acting President.

Section 4. Whenever the Vice President and a majority of either the principal officers of the executive departments or of such other body as Congress may by law provide, transmit to the President pro tempore of the Senate and the Speaker of the House of Representatives their written declaration that the President is unable to discharge the powers and duties of his office, the Vice President shall immediately assume the powers and duties of the office as Acting President.

Thereafter, when the President transmits to the President pro tempore of the Senate and the Speaker of the House of Representatives has written declaration that no inability exists, he shall resume the powers and duties of his office unless the Vice President and a majority of either the principal officers of the executive departments or of such other body as Congress may by law provide, transmit within four days to the President pro tempore of the Senate and the Speaker of the House of Representatives their written declaration that the President is unable to discharge the powers and duties of his office. Thereupon Congress shall decide the issue, assembling within forty-eight hours for that purpose if not in session. If the Congress, within twenty-one days after receipt of the latter written declaration, or, if Congress is not in session, within twenty-one days after Congress is required to assemble, determines by two-thirds vote of both Houses that the President is unable to discharge the powers and duties of his office, the Vice President shall continue to discharge the same as Acting President; otherwise, the President shall resume the powers and duties of his office.

Amendment XXVI
[June 30, 1971]

Section 1. The right of citizens of the United States, who are eighteen years of age or older, to vote shall not be denied or abridged by the United States or any State on account of age.

Section 2. The Congress shall have the power to enforce this article by appropriate legislation.

Index